THEMATIC UNIT
Ladybugs

Written by Dona Herweck Rice

Teacher Created Materials, Inc.
6421 Industry Way
Westminster, CA 92683
www.teachercreated.com
©1999 Teacher Created Materials, Inc.
Reprinted, 2004
Made in U.S.A.
ISBN-1-57690-370-2

Illustrator:
Barb Lorseyedi

Editor:
Janet A. Hale, M.S. Ed.

Cover Artist:
Cheri Macoubrie Wilson

Table of Contents

Introduction

Ladybugs is a comprehensive thematic unit that uses the friendly, helpful beetles as a basis for lessons across the curriculum. Its eighty pages are filled with a variety of activities, plans, and management tools that are sure to interest and motivate primary children while easing the teacher's workload. This literature-based thematic unit uses two high-quality selections at its core: *The Grouchy Ladybug* by Eric Carle and *The Ladybug and Other Insects: A First Discovery Book* by Gallimard Jeunesse and Pascale de Bourgoing. The children will experience the various essential content areas through activities that connect each work of literature across the curriculum. In addition, many of the activities can be done cooperatively, enhancing everyone's learning experience.

This thematic unit includes the following:

❏ **literature selections**—summaries of two children's books with related lessons (complete with reproducible pages) that cross the curriculum

❏ **planning guides**—suggestions for introducing the unit, sequencing the lessons, and making projects and displays

❏ **curriculum connections**—activities in language arts, math, science, social studies, art, music, physical education, and life skills that you can incorporate into your daily curriculum

❏ **unit management suggestions**—teacher aids for organizing the unit, including incentives, patterns, and a unit award

❏ **culminating activity**—class activity that will enrich the classroom experience and synthesize the learning

❏ **bibliography**—suggested additional readings relating to the theme

---

To keep this valuable resource intact so that it can be used year after year, you may wish to punch holes in the pages and store them in a three-ring binder.

Introduction (cont.)

Why a Balanced Approach?

The strength of a whole language approach is that it involves children in using all modes of communication: reading, writing, listening, illustrating, and doing. Communication skills are interconnected and integrated into lessons that emphasize the whole of language. Balancing this approach is our knowledge that every whole—including individual words—is composed of parts, and directed study of those parts can help a child to master the whole. Experience and research tell us that regular attention to phonics, other word-attack skills, spelling, and so forth, develops reading mastery, thereby fulfilling the unity of the whole-language experience. The child is thus led to read, write, spell, speak, and listen confidently in response to a literature experience introduced by the teacher. In these ways, language skills grow rapidly, stimulated by direct practice, involvement, and interest in the topic at hand.

Why Thematic Planning?

One very useful tool for implementing a balanced language program is thematic planning. By choosing a theme with correlating literature selections for a unit of study, a teacher can plan activities throughout the day that lead to a cohesive, in-depth study of the topic. Children will be practicing and applying their skills in meaningful contexts. Consequently, they tend to learn and retain more. Both teachers and children will be freed from a day that is broken into unrelated segments of isolated drill and practice.

Why Cooperative Learning?

Besides academic skills and content, children need to learn social skills. No longer can this area of development be taken for granted. Children must learn to work cooperatively in groups in order to function well in modern society. Group activities should be a regular part of school life, and teachers should consciously include social objectives as well as academic objectives in their planning. For example, a group working together to write a report may need to select a leader. The teacher should make clear to the children and monitor the qualities of good leader-follower group interactions, just as he or she would state and monitor the academic goals of the project.

Why Big Books?

An excellent, cooperative, whole-language activity is the production of Big Books. Groups of children, or the whole class, can apply their language skills, content knowledge, and creativity to produce a Big Book that can become a part of the classroom library to be read and reread. These books make excellent culminating projects for sharing beyond the classroom with parents, librarians, other classes, and so forth. Big Books can be produced in many ways, and this thematic unit book includes directions for at least one method you may choose.

The Grouchy Ladybug

by Eric Carle

Summary

Whoever heard of a grouchy ladybug? Ladybugs are friendly and helpful, right? Wrong! In Eric Carle's classic story, the title character is a grouchy old pest who threatens to fight his fellow creatures rather than to share his food. When another ladybug lands on the aphid-covered leaf the Grouchy Ladybug wants, he tries to pick a fight, but backs off when the other bug agrees to brawl. Throughout the day, the ladybug flies from creature to creature, looking for a fight; however, when each is willing to comply, the bug simply claims, "Oh, you're not big enough," and off he flies. Finally, he cannot fly away from his largest foe, a blue whale who bats away the bug with a flick of his giant tail. The ladybug lands right back where he started, but this time he is more than willing to share the aphids with the friendly ladybug. Together they eat all the insect pests and then fall off to sleep.

Eric Carle's creative tale is told with his trademark collage illustrations and die-cut pages. Not only is the story delightful to read, but it is a pleasure to look at as well. Children will especially enjoy the small clock in the corner of each page which keeps time throughout the Grouchy Ladybug's busy day.

Sample Plan

Lesson 1

- Send home a letter to the parents (page 73).
- Do one or more prereading activities (page 6).
- Read aloud *The Grouchy Ladybug*.
- Discuss the book (page 6).
- Explore at a Ladybug Observation Center (pages 57–58).
- Decorate the room with ladybugs (page 75).
- Create a class graph (page 6).

Lesson 2

- Test story comprehension with Who Is It? (page 8).
- Host an interview with the Grouchy Ladybug (page 7).
- Relate favorite parts of the story (page 9).
- Practice telling time (pages 10 and 11).
- Complete ladybug word problems (page 40).
- Move with Ladybug Life Cycle Lines (page 66).

Lesson 3

- Compare relative times (page 12).
- Allow children to tell about their own grouchy days (page 16).
- Make an art project in the style of Eric Carle (page 18).
- Complete a ladybug writing activity (page 32).
- Practice shape words and recognition (page 44).

- Practice map skills with Follow That Bug! (page 53)

Lesson 4

- Make ladybug clocks (pages 13–15)
- Complete the ladybug crossword (page 37).
- Order the ladybugs from least to most (pages 41–42).
- Make ladybug apple snacks (page 69).
- Move with Ladybug Facts (pages 66 and 68).
- Take a look at the ladybug life cycle (pages 59–60).

Lesson 5

- Match feelings and their expressions (page 17).
- Color bookmarks (page 74) and have children create their own.
- Complete a ladybug writing activity (page 33).
- Practice facts for the number twenty (page 43).
- Make thumbprint art projects (page 64).

Lesson 6

- Share some ladybug poetry (page 39).
- Play The Ladybug Game (pages 47–48).
- Complete a math activity (pages 51–52).
- Make a ladybug cake (page 70).
- Make invitations to a culminating party (pages 71–72).

Overview of Activities

Setting the Stage

1. Before you begin reading the book with your children, do some prereading activities to stimulate interest and enhance comprehension. Some activities you might try include:
   - Predict what the story might be about by reading the title and looking at the cover picture.
   - Children might be familiar with other books by Eric Carle. Have the children relate other Eric Carle books with which they are familiar.
   - Answer some reading-interest questions:
       Do you like bugs?
       Are you interested in stories about animals? About ladybugs?
       Have you ever felt grouchy?

2. Create a class graph. To do so, make two columns on a sheet of butcher paper. At the top, write the question, "Who Likes Bugs?" Write, "I Do," above one column and, "I Don't," above the other. Give each child a ladybug to color. (Use the pattern on page 41 or page 51.) Instruct the children to place their bugs in the appropriate column of the graph, using tape. Ask the children to tell you if there is more liking of bugs in the class or more disliking. As other teachers, children, and parents visit your room, add their opinions to your graph and see how the graph results change. (Make this a lesson in tallying by counting the bugs by ones and fives.)

Enjoying the Book

1. Read *The Grouchy Ladybug* aloud to your class. Use variety and expression in your voice, engaging the children by your reading as well as the words. If desired, encourage the children to predict what might happen as you read aloud; however, it may prove more desirable to read the book through without interruption, allowing the children to experience the story as a whole and to engage their own thoughts about what they hear.
2. After the reading, discuss the book with the children. Ask if they have ever seen any of the creatures mentioned in the book. Allow them to share their stories and how they compare to the Grouchy Ladybug's experiences.
3. Share the book a second time, this time allowing the children to match the creatures and their actions (page 8). Alternatively, they can complete this activity individually or as a class after the reading as an exercise in reading comprehension.
4. Pretend that the Grouchy Ladybug is visiting your classroom. Have the children answer the following questions according to how the bug might answer them:
   - What do you like to do all day?
   - What would a happy day for you be like?
   - What would it be like if you came to our classroom as a child?
   - What would it be like if we played together as friends?
5. Have each child pick his or her favorite part of the book and illustrate it on page 9. Afterwards, have the children share their pictures and tell about their favorite parts. They can also make a graph showing their favorites.
6. Everyone gets grouchy now and then. Let the children tell about their grouchy days by completing the activity on page 16. Extend the activity by letting them tell about a friendly day, a sad day, an angry day, and so on.

Overview of Activities *(cont.)*

Extending the Book

1. Program the time sheet (page 11) to match the skills you are teaching (hour hand, minute hand, half hours, etc.). You can either fill in the hands of the clock and have the children write in the times or fill in the times and have the children draw in the hands. You can also test both skills by doing some of each. Provide the children with page 10 for instruction and review.

2. When completing page 12, let the children know that the times they choose may vary from those of other people. After they are finished, share the answers as a class, discussing which times are likeliest.

3. Continue your study of time by making and using clocks (pages 13–15). Test the children by having them move the hands of the clocks to times you call out. They can also use their clocks to test one another.

4. As a class, discuss the feelings in the book. Then complete the activity on page 17, allowing children to share about their own feelings and to experiment with all kinds of "feeling" art.

5. When doing the activity on page 18, provide other samples of Eric Carle's work for the children to see.

6. Make mobiles based on the book. Let children draw pictures of each animal the ladybug meets in the story. Cut out these pictures and suspend them from a hanger. Then have the children draw the ladybug. Attach the ladybug to a paper clip. Let the children retell the story, moving the paper clip ladybug to each animal as he or she tells that part of the story.

7. A few children at a time can play Grouchy Ladybug Lotto. Make several lotto gameboards by dividing construction paper into four squares. On each square, include a picture of an animal from *The Grouchy Ladybug*. (Use a clip art book or make simple line sketches based on the drawings in the book.) Each gameboard should be unique with a different combination of animals. Make game cards in the same way, but cut the four squares apart. Shuffle the cards and place them face down in a pile. Let children take turns drawing the cards. If the animal card matches an animal on the child's gameboard, he or she can place the card face up on the gameboard. If the animal does not match any of the animals on the gameboard, the card is returned to the bottom of the pile. The first child to fill up his or her gameboard wins the game.

8. After completing the writing activities on pages 32–36, allow the children to share what they have written. If desired, bind their writings together into class books or have individual children bind their own writings into books for themselves. Display these books during your culminating activity (pages 71–72).

9. When sharing ladybug poetry (page 39), let the children cut out big leaves from construction paper. Provide them with duplicated copies of each of the poems or let them copy them themselves. Glue a poem to each leaf. Decorate the leaves with ladybugs.

10. To use the open worksheet on pages 51–52, simply fill in problems from any math skill you wish to study or review. The worksheet can also be used for other subject areas. For example, children can match synonyms (language arts) or match cities with states or provinces (social studies). The uses are endless.

Directions: Read ̄ ̄ ̄ ̄ ̄ ̄ ̄ ̄ ̄ ̄ ̄ ̄ ̄ ̄ ̄ ̄ s to their actions by writing their names in the blank

_____ 1. beats

_____ 2. lifts i

_____ 3. rais

_____ 4. opens its jaws

_____ 5. lowers its horn

_____ 6. gives a slap

_____ 7. shows its stinger

_____ 8. opens its beak

_____ 9. laughs and shows its teeth

_____ 10. reaches out its legs

_____ 11. offers to share

_____ 12. stretches its claws

elephant	ladybug	rhinoceros	stag beetle
gorilla	lobster	skunk	whale
hyena	praying mantis	sparrow	yellow jacket

Challenge: What animal in the book is missing from this list?

My Favorite Part

Directions: After reading *The Grouchy Ladybug*, write about your favorite part. Draw a picture to show what happens.

My favorite part of the book is when _____

_____

_____

_____

_____

_____

_____

_____

_____

Telling Time

Learning to tell time is like playing a game. You have to be able to read numbers on a clock's face by the positions of the clock's hands.

This is the face of a clock. The face has the numbers 1 to 12 written on it.

These are the hands of a clock. The hand that measures minutes is longer than the hand that measures hours.

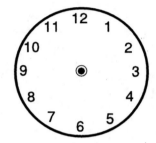

Each hour is marked on the clock in a special way. The minute hand points to twelve, and the hour hand points to the hour it is.

Half hours are marked on the clock with the minute hand pointing to the six and the hour hand halfway between two numbers.

Quarter hours are marked on the clock with the minute hand pointing either to the three or to the nine. The hour hand is either one-fourth or three-fourths past the hour number.

Knowing how to tell time is very important. It is lots of fun, too!

10

Telling Time *(cont.)*

Directions: Show that you understand how to tell time by completing the times below.

Teacher Note: See page 7, #1.

How Long?

Directions: Can these things best be measured by seconds, minutes, or hours? Write your answer on each of the blanks below.

1. How long does it take to brush your hair?

    _____

2. How long does it take to clean your room?

    _____

3. How long does it take to climb a tree?

    _____

4. How long does it take to tie your shoes?

    _____

5. How long does it take to draw a picture? _____

6. How long does it take to eat your breakfast? _____

7. How long does it take to make a paper airplane? _____

8. How long does it take to get a good night's sleep? _____

9. How long does it take to sneeze? _____

10. How long does it take to watch a cartoon? _____

11. How long does it take to make a sandwich? _____

12. How long does it take to give a hug? _____

13. How long does it take to play a game of baseball? _____

14. How long does it take to read a comic strip? _____

15. How long does it take to fly around the world? _____

Clockmakers

Ladybug clocks are an excellent way to practice time-telling skills while studying *The Grouchy Ladybug*. Follow these directions.

Materials:

- patterns (page 14–15)
- red and black construction paper
- white index paper
- pencils

- scissors
- glue
- brass fasteners
- black and red markers

Directions:

1. Duplicate the clock and clock hands patterns onto white index paper and cut them out. Color the hands black or red.

2. Trace the wing patterns onto red construction paper and cut them out.

3. Trace the ladybug head and shield pattern onto black construction paper and cut it out.

4. Color symmetrical black dot patterns on each of the wings.

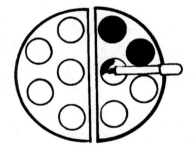

5. Use a brass fastener to affix the hands to the clock face, aligning the dots.

6. Affix the wings at the dots to the clock, again using brass fasteners.

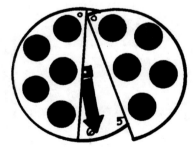

7. Glue the head and shield to the clock body by attaching it to the underside of the body.

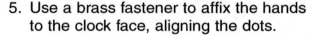

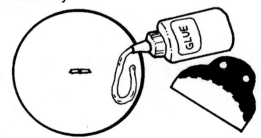

8. Open the wings and tell the time! Use the clock while re-reading *The Grouchy Ladybug*, matching your ladybug clock's time to the book's time.

Clockmakers *(cont.)*

clock/body

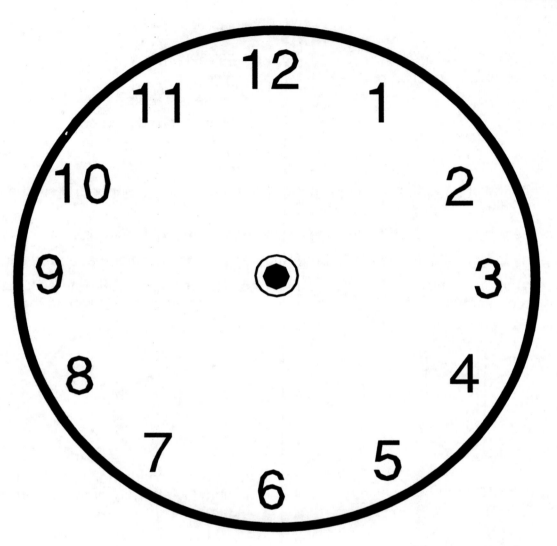

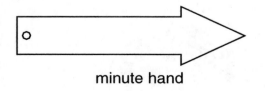

minute hand

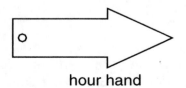

hour hand

Clockmakers *(cont.)*

wings

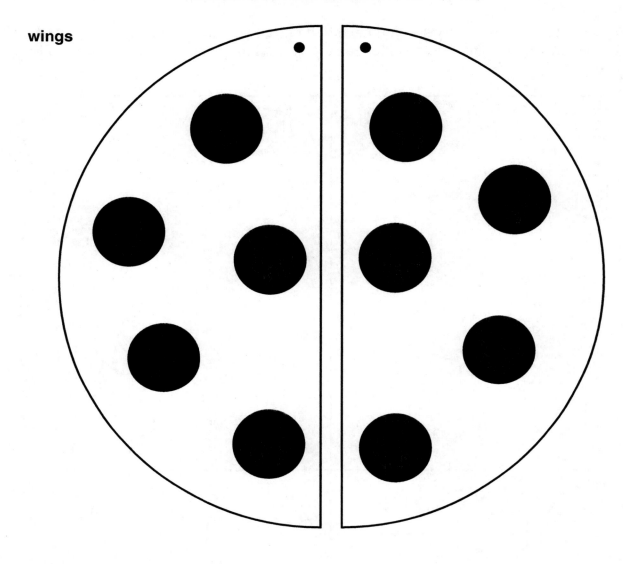

head and shield

My Grouchy Day

Directions: Tell about a grouchy day you have had or that you can imagine. Fill in the times on the clocks and the blanks. Write sentences to tell what happened and draw pictures to go with the words.

Feelings

Directions: *The Grouchy Ladybug's* feelings change from grouchy to friendly and grateful. Match the feelings below to the faces that show them. Then try drawing the feeling faces yourself.

Your Turn

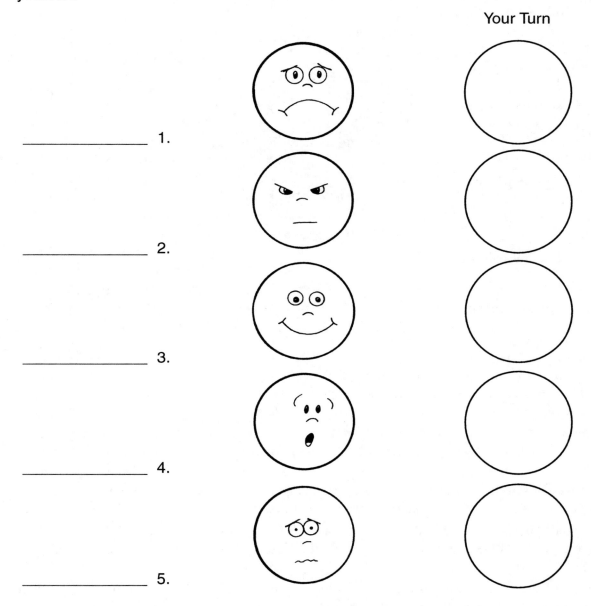

_____ 1.

_____ 2.

_____ 3.

_____ 4.

_____ 5.

happy	sad	angry	surprised	confused

Challenge: Can you draw a grouchy face?

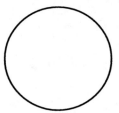

The Art of Eric Carle

Eric Carle is a world-famous illustrator of children's books. Part of the reason why is his distinctive, bold, and colorful artwork. One technique for which he is perhaps most famous is that of tissue paper collage or overlay. Allow your children to experiment with the artistic style of Eric Carle by doing some tissue paper collages of their own.

Materials:

- colored tissue paper
- paintbrushes (various sizes)
- liquid laundry starch
- plastic cups
- sturdy white drawing paper
- pencils
- scissors
- crayons, markers, and paints
- smocks
- newspapers or plastic table covers

Directions:

1. Sketch a simple scene or object onto the paper, filling the page. A basic landscape is a good idea. For example, just three curved lines across the paper can become sea, land, and sky when the colors are added.

2. Work from one end of the picture across or from the inside out. Do not try to work in many directions at once. Also, do not place light colored tissue on top of dark since it will virtually disappear.

3. Once you have chosen the area in which you wish to begin, wet a brush of the appropriate size with a small amount of starch. Spread the starch in that area.

4. Tear a few small pieces of tissue in the color or colors desired. Overlap them in the correct area. Cover them with a bit more starch to make them stick. (Use scissors for cutting precise shapes in the tissue.)

5. Cover the rest of the picture in the same way, adding starch as needed. Be sure to put starch down first so that the tissue sticks well, but do not use too much starch because it will make the colors run.

6. For an added effect, use the color that comes off on the brush to help fill in the background of the picture or scene.

7. When it is complete, lay the picture somewhere to dry. Drying time will depend on the amount of starch used.

8. When it is dry, add details with crayons, markers, or paints.

The Ladybug and Other Insects

by Gallimard Jeunesse and Pascale de Bourgoing

Summary

This engaging, non-fiction book provides interesting facts about ladybugs accompanied by realistic, detailed illustrations. Worth particular note is the use of clear plastic overlays, allowing the reader to see inside and beneath certain illustrations. For example, while first we see a woodpecker pecking at a tree, when we lift the overlay we see ladybugs hibernating inside. While the majority of the book is about ladybugs, the last few pages provide information and illustrations on insects in general.

Sample Plan

Lesson 1

- Complete one or more prereading activities (page 20).
- Read and discuss *The Ladybug and Other Insects.*
- Make a "What We Know" chart (page 20).
- Send a letter from an aphid to a ladybug (page 20).
- Use ladybugs to learn about hundreds (page 21).
- Complete the comprehension activity on pages 22–23.

Lesson 2

- Study the eating method of ladybugs (page 21).
- Make overlays like those found in the book (page 24).
- Complete a ladybug writing activity (page 34).
- Learn about symmetry (page 45).
- Label the parts of a ladybug (page 54).
- Make a ladybug magnet or pin (page 65).
- Play Ladybug, May I? (page 67).

Lesson 3

- Study the hibernation of ladybugs (page 21).
- Create ladybug puppets (page 25).
- Take a look at the ladybug life cycle (pages 20; 30–31).
- Do the wordsearch (page 38).

- Practice matching equal numbers (page 46).
- Enjoy some ladybug ice cream (page 69).

Lesson 4

- Learn more about ladybug colors (page 29).
- Complete a ladybug writing activity (pages 35–36).
- Crack the number code (page 49).
- Learn about the food chain (pages 55–56).
- Play Food Chain Freeze Tag (page 67).

Lesson 5

- Go on a ladybug hunt (page 21).
- Take what has been learned to create ladybug fact books (pages 26–27).
- Review math skills with a pencil poke (page 50).
- Study the traits of insects (pages 61–63).
- Make a ladybug clip (page 65).

Lesson 6

- Study ladybug antennae and how they work (page 21).
- Share some ladybug poetry (page 39).
- Complete a math activity (pages 51–52).
- Create a ladybug crayon relief picture (page 65).
- Have a ladybug culminating party, including a ladybug ball (pages 71–72).
- Give unit awards (page 78).

Overview of Activities

Setting the Stage
---

1. Before you begin reading the book with your children, do some prereading activities to stimulate interest and enhance comprehension. Some activities you might try include: predict what the book might be about by reading the title and looking at the cover picture; brainstorm for what the children already know about ladybugs and insects in general; and answer some reading-interest questions:

   - Have you ever studied an insect up close? How about a ladybug?
   - Do you like insects? Why or why not?
   - What is the most beautiful or unusual insect you have ever seen?

2. Tell children about aphids and how they survive. Let children know that aphids are a main source of food for ladybugs. Instruct the children to write a letter from an aphid to a ladybug, using the information they have learned about aphids and ladybugs. Let them use the stationery paper on page 77. (After reading the book, have them write a letter in reply.)

Enjoying the Book
---

1. Read *The Ladybug and Other Insects* aloud. If desired, encourage the children to predict what might happen as you read aloud; however, it may prove more desirable to read the book through without interruption, allowing the children to experience the story as a whole and to engage their own thoughts about what they hear.

2. After the reading, discuss the book with the children. Ask if they have ever observed a ladybug up close. Allow them to relate their stories and to compare what they observed with the information and pictures in the book.

3. Make the ladybug puppets on page 25. Then reread the book, letting the children work as puppeteers to mimic the ladybug activities described in the book.

4. Let the children show their comprehension of the book by completing the activity on pages 22–23. You can also make a class chart. Write "What We Know About Ladybugs" at the top of a sheet of butcher paper. Underneath, write everything the children say they know about ladybugs. Attach child-made drawings of ladybugs (cut out) all around the margins and laminate your chart for display.

   Another way to demonstrate comprehension is to make fact books. A variety of methods can be found on pages 26–28. The pages include a list of ladybug facts, several of which are not included in *The Ladybug and Other Insects*.

5. To extend the life cycle activity on pages 30–31, cover the pictures on page 31 when duplicating it. Then have the children draw in the life-cycle stages themselves. Another life cycle activity can be found on pages 59–60, and the following instructions are for a third method:

   Cut out two circles of the same size. Draw lines dividing each circle into quarters. On the first circle, write the number one in the top left section near the center folds, mark a 2 in the top right section, a 3 in the bottom right, and a 4 in the bottom left. On the second circle, continue in the same way but with the numbers 5, 6, 7, and 8. Cut a radius from each circle along the fold between sections 1 and 4, 5 and 8.

Overview of Activities *(cont.)*

Enjoying the Book *(cont.)*

Draw, color, and label a picture in each circle section, following the life cycle of a ladybug. Complete the drawings as follows: (1) adult ladybug, (2) eggs, (3) larvae, (4) first molting, (5) second molting, (6) third molting, (7) pupa, (8) adult ladybug.

Lay down the first circle, drawings up, and place the second circle on top of it with drawings up and the cut side matching the first. Tape section 5 to section 4 along the cut so that section 5 continues naturally from section 4. Fold section 8 over on top of section 7, fold the two sections up over section 6, and then fold the three sections across over section 5. Next, fold those four sections down over section 4, across over section 3, up over section 2, and finally across over section 1. You should now have a little book in the shape of a quarter circle. Turn the book over so that the back side of section 1 is facing you and write a book title (such as Ladybug Life Cycle). Open the page and unfold in progression to read the book.

5. Study the science behind ladybugs. To do so, provide a variety of resource books on the topic. (See the bibliography, page 79.) Let children work as partners or groups to find out how ladybugs eat, how their feelers work, what happens when they hibernate, and more. When you find the answers, let the children make posters that explain the science. Display the posters around your room. (If such research is too elevated for your children to do, lead them in a class study. Then let them make the corresponding posters.)

6. Have each child pick his or her favorite part of the book and illustrate it. Use the form on page 9, changing the directions as needed. Afterwards, have the children share their pictures and tell about their favorite parts. They can also make a graph, showing their favorites.

Extending the Book

1. Use ladybugs to learn about hundreds. To do so, punch out 100 yellow circles to represent ladybug eggs and 100 green to represent aphids. (You can also use green and yellow dried beans or hard candies.) Let the children count and group the eggs and aphids. Let them know that a ladybug can lay up to 100 eggs at a time and eat up to 100 aphids in a day. Although these numbers are higher than the average, they are still possible.

2. Go on a ladybug hunt. Duplicate and cut out several sets of ladybugs from page 75. Hide them all around the room, adding a few leaves, paper aphids, or other items with them. Create the illusion of ladybugs in natural settings. Then let the children hunt for the ladybugs. Afterwards, they can write sentences about what the ladybugs were "doing" when they found them.

3. When completing the activity on pages 35–36, you might wish to have the children draw "beliefs" from a hat. This is also a good writing activity for partners or small groups.

4. After completing the activity on page 49, have the children color the ladybugs. The ashy gray ladybug is gray with black spots. The others can be colored red with black spots and black and white markings on the head. Orange and yellow are also common colors and can be used as desired. Note: This activity can be done in conjunction with page 29.

5. To use pages 51–52, write a math problem on each ladybug spot. Write the answers on the spots on the next page. Instruct the children to cut out and glue the spots in their correct places. Change the activity as needed to review different math skills. The pages can be used for other areas of the curriculum as well.

Interesting Things About Ladybugs

After reading *The Ladybug and Other Insects*, have the children complete the following comprehension activity.

Materials

- ladybug patterns (page 23)
- 11" x 17" (28 cm x 43 cm) green construction paper
- red, black, white, yellow, and orange felt
- lined writing paper
- scissors
- pencils or pens
- craft, fabric, or tacky glue
- crayons or markers

Directions

1. Independently, or as a class, brainstorm for interesting facts about ladybugs. These should be taken from the book, but children can also add other facts they know about ladybugs. Each child should neatly write a list of these interesting facts on a sheet of lined paper.

2. Glue each sheet of lined paper to the bottom half of a sheet of green construction paper, leaving the top half empty.

3. Provide each child with a set of ladybug patterns.

4. Allow each child to choose ladybug colors from the available felt. The chosen colors should reflect actual ladybug color combinations. Have the children trace their patterns onto the felt and then cut out the pieces. (They can cut tiny strips of black felt to make the antennae.)

5. Each child should glue his or her ladybug pattern pieces to the top half of the green paper, constructing a fabric ladybug.

6. The children can add scenery details (such as leaves, twigs, and aphids) around the ladybug, using crayons or markers.

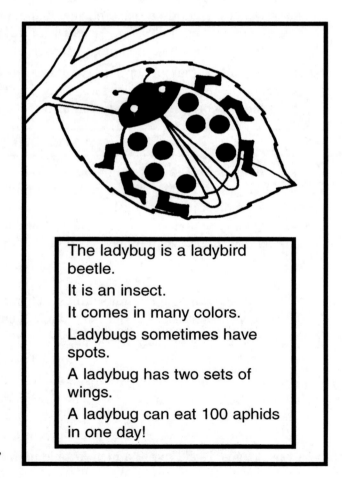

The ladybug is a ladybird beetle.

It is an insect.

It comes in many colors.

Ladybugs sometimes have spots.

A ladybug has two sets of wings.

A ladybug can eat 100 aphids in one day!

22

Interesting Things About
Ladybugs *(cont.)*

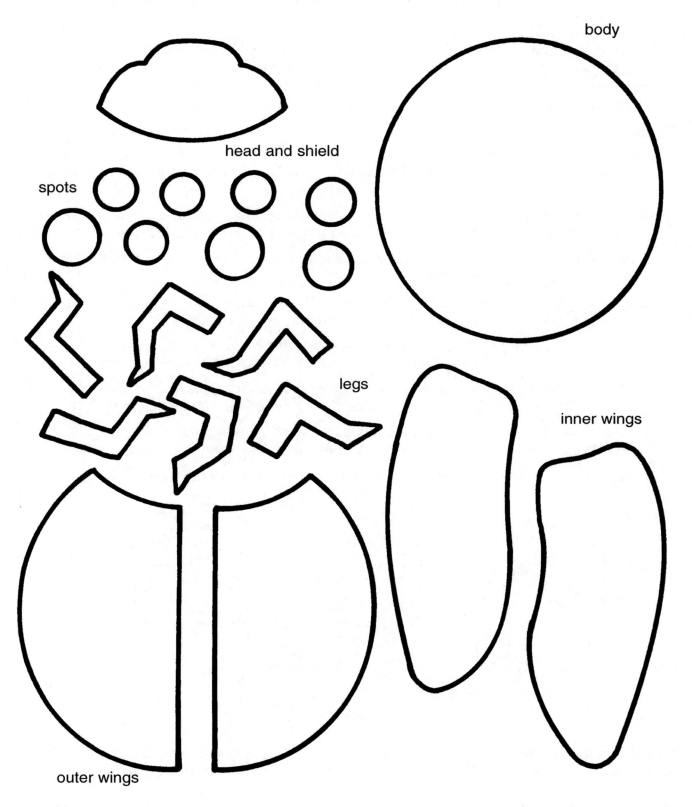

body

head and shield

spots

legs

inner wings

outer wings

Ladybug Overlays

Part of the interest in *The Ladybug and Other Insects* is the use of clear overlays. The children can make ladybug overlays of their own by following these directions.

Materials

- white index paper
- white drawing paper
- patterns (page 23)
- sturdy, clear plastic wrap

- crayons
- scissors
- pencils
- stapler

Directions

1. Look at pages 9–11 of the book. (The pages are unnumbered. Count from the title page.) These show a ladybug in flight and at rest. You will make your own versions of this page.

2. Trace and cut one body pattern, one set of leg patterns, two sets of outer wing patterns, one set of inner wing patterns, and one head and shield on the drawing paper.

3. Color the body, the head and shield, and the legs black. Leave the inner wings white. Color the outer wings red with black spots.

4. On a sheet of index paper, construct a ladybug at rest, using one set of outer wings, the head and shield, and the legs. Draw on the antennae and eyes.

5. Cut out a 1" (2.5 cm) border around two sheets of index paper, leaving the center of each empty. Cut a sheet of plastic wrap the same size as the borders.

6. Glue the plastic wrap between the index paper borders. You now have a clear sheet with a paper border on both sides. Lay this sheet over the sheet with the ladybug at rest.

7. On the plastic sheet, directly over the ladybug at rest, glue on the ladybug body, inner wings, and a second set of outer wings plus the spots, showing the ladybug in flight.

8. Staple the two sheets together along the left margin. You now have a completed overlay.

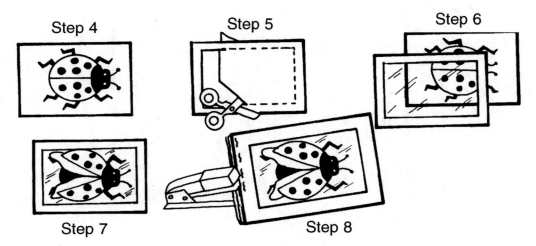

Step 4   Step 5   Step 6

Step 7   Step 8

You can use this overlay method for many other things. Let the children brainstorm for other overlay ideas and then make the overlays individually or with a partner to share with the class.

Ladybug Puppet

Make a simple ladybug puppet by following these directions.

Materials:

- body pattern
- red, black, and white felt
- red or black sewing thread or embroidery thread
- large sewing needles
- fabric, craft, or tacky glue
- scissors
- white chalk

Directions:

1. Using white chalk, trace the entire pattern (head and body) onto black felt, marking the "leg" holes. (See position of "leg" holes on pattern.) Cut out the holes and the body piece. This will make the bottom of the body.

2. Again using the white chalk, trace only the body pattern onto red felt. Cut it out.

3. Cut out the head piece from the pattern and trace it onto black felt. To make the eyes, cut two small circles from white felt and glue them to the head. Cut out the head and glue it in the appropriate place on the red felt to make the upper body.

4. Cut out a strip of black felt to glue along the center of the upper body to divide the wings. Also cut out black dots to decorate the wings with spots.

5. Place the upper body on top of the lower body and stitch them together around the sides and head. Leave the tail-end free.

6. Place your hand inside the puppet, inserting your fingers through the holes. You now have a ladybug puppet!

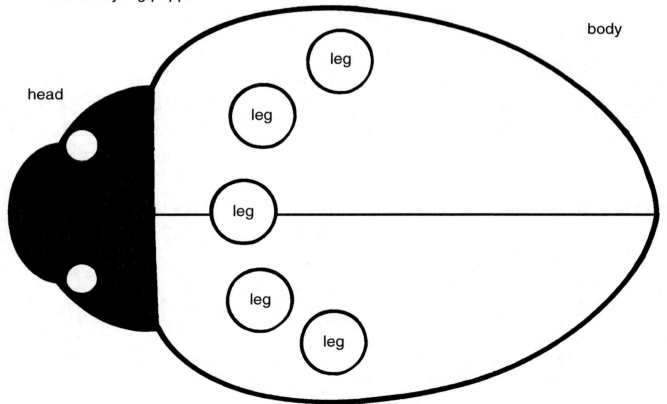

Fact Book

Let the children collect their new knowledge in ladybug fact books. There are many ways to make fact books, and below are just a few examples. On the next page are patterns for making one version, and on page 28 are a list of ladybug facts. Use these facts together with the information in *The Ladybug and Other Insects* to fill in the content of your books. Children can also research ladybugs in other resources, and the bibliography on page 79 will give you many good ideas.

Big Books

Let children work in pairs or small groups to construct a page for a class big book. Each page should contain an important ladybug fact with corresponding illustration(s). Make a cover and title page for the book, allowing each child to sign his or her name.

On the Dot

Cut a large ladybug body from red (or yellow, orange, etc.) construction paper. Cut a head and stripe from black construction paper and glue them to the body. (The stripe will make the wings.) Write ladybug facts on small circles of paper and glue these circles in a symmetrical pattern on the ladybug's wings. Cover each fact with a circular flap of black construction paper, glued at the top so they can be lifted to read the facts below.

Facts in Flight

Cut a large ladybug body from white paper and two red (or yellow, orange, etc.) wings. Glue a head made from black paper to the top of the body. Affix the wings to the body with brass fasteners at the top (so that the wings will open). On the body, write a list of ladybug facts. On the wings, color black dots and add a book title.

Take to Wing

Using the patterns on page 27, duplicate the body pattern once on black paper, the wing pattern twice on red, yellow, or orange paper, and the wing pattern on white paper as many times as necessary. Take half of the white wings and place them with their flat sides to the right. Take the other half and place the flat sides to the left, making an equal number of wings facing each direction. Write a ladybug fact on each white wing. Cover each stack of wings with a colored wing. Punch a hole through each stack. Attach the wing stacks to the body, using brass fasteners through the holes. Decorate the colored wings with black dots and a book title.

Fact Book *(cont.)*

See page 26 for suggested uses.

body

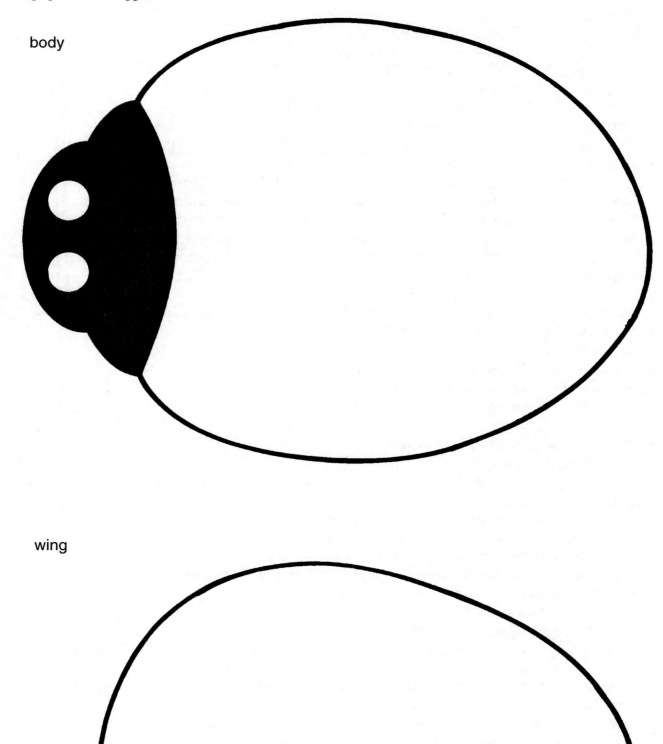

wing

Fact Book *(cont.)*

- A ladybug is a beetle.
- Ladybugs are insects.
- Ladybugs are both male and female.
- The real name for a ladybug is a ladybird beetle.
- Ladybugs have three main body parts: abdomen, thorax (shield), and head.
- Ladybugs have six legs.
- At the end of each ladybug leg is a claw and a sticky pad.
- Ladybugs use their legs for walking, climbing, and cleaning themselves.
- Ladybugs have two sets of wings. Only the inner wings move during flight.
- Ladybugs are not good fliers. They like walking best.
- Ladybugs eat harmful pests in gardens and orchards and on farms.
- Ladybugs come in many colors, especially red, orange, yellow, and black.
- There are more than 4,000 kinds of ladybugs. About 350 kinds live in North America.
- Predators do not like to eat ladybugs because they taste bad and have a hard shell. Some people believe that their bright colors also frighten predators.
- Ladybugs have strong jaws.
- Ladybugs eat their prey by grabbing it in their jaws, filling it with a juice that turns the inside of the prey's body into liquid, and then sucking the liquid from its body.
- A ladybug's favorite food is an aphid.
- Ladybugs can eat up to 100 aphids in one day.
- Just one dozen ladybugs can save a fruit tree from ruin by insect pests.
- Ladybugs lay 10 to 100 eggs at one time.
- Ladybugs lay their eggs on leaves, especially the leaves with plenty of aphids for their grubs (babies) to eat.
- Ladybug eggs are sticky and yellow.
- Ladybug eggs turn white in five days.
- Ladybugs go through a metamorphosis as they grow from egg to larva to pupa and then adult.
- A ladybug larva is about the size of a pinhead.
- A ladybug larva molts its skin three times while it grows.
- After a ladybug larva has grown for 3 to 4 weeks, it attaches itself upside down under a leaf, sheds its skin, and becomes a pupa. The new skin forms a hard, protective case around the pupa.
- New ladybugs have no spots.
- Some ladybugs never have spots.
- When a new ladybug emerges, it is wet. As soon as it has dried, its spots appear, and it can fly.
- Ladybugs hibernate in groups during the winter. Their hibernation is also called diapause.
- Ladybugs mate in the spring. Mating can last for up to 2 hours.
- Ladybugs are named for Mary, the mother of Jesus, who some people call Our Lady.
- Many people think that ladybugs are good luck. In the past, many people believed that they had magical powers.

Lovely Ladybug Colors

Directions: Ladybugs come in many colors. Crack the color code by writing the letter in each blank that *comes before* the letter given in the alphabet. For example, if the letter given is D, then write C in the blank. Then color the ladybugs.

1. ___ ___ ___   and   ___ ___ ___ ___ ___
   S F E   C M B D L

2. ___ ___ ___ ___ ___ ___   and   ___ ___ ___ ___ ___ ___
   P S B O H F   Z F M M P X

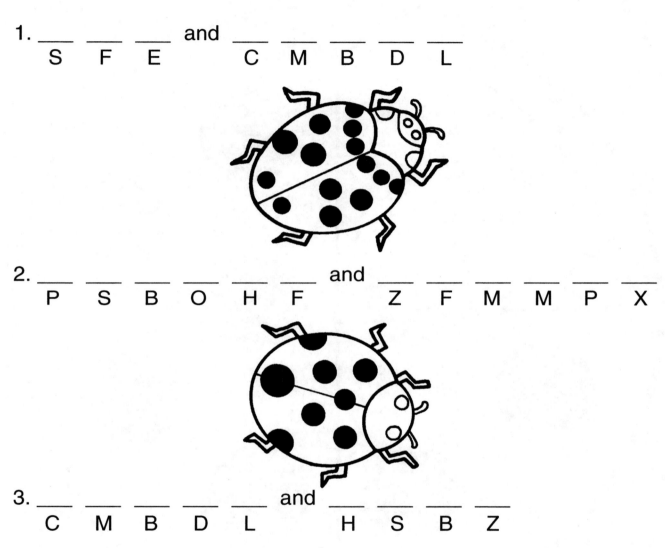

3. ___ ___ ___ ___ ___   and   ___ ___ ___ ___
   C M B D L   H S B Z

A B C D E F G H I J K L M N O P Q R S T U V W X Y Z

    29

Life Cycle 1

Directions: Color and cut out the ladybug below and the life cycle wheel on the next page. Cut out the window in the ladybug. Fasten the wheel behind the ladybug with a brass fastener through the center holes. The life cycle stages will show through the ladybug's body when the wheel is turned.

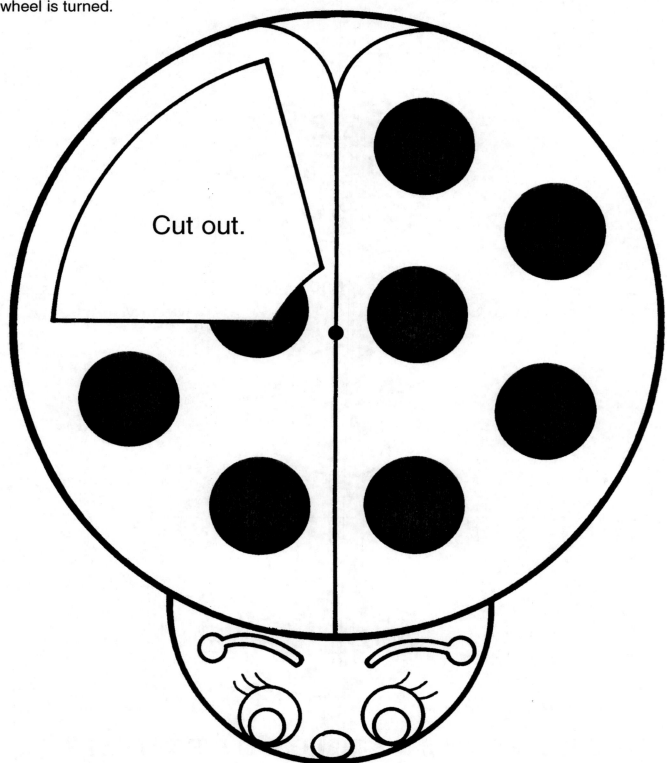

Cut out.

30

Life Cycle 1 *(cont.)*

See page 30 for use.

Ladybug Legs

Everyone might guess that a ladybug uses its legs to walk and to climb, but ladybugs also use their legs for something surprising. Can you guess what it is? Ladybugs use their legs to clean themselves! First, a ladybug nibbles dirt from its two front legs. Then it rubs its middle legs and back legs together to clean them. Finally, it uses its back legs to clean its inner wings by rubbing them against its outer wings. Amazing, isn't it?

Directions: What can you do with your legs? Use your thinking skills and your imagination to make a list of all the things you can do with your legs. Write your list here.

How the Ladybug Got Its Name

During the Middle Ages a long time ago, many people were farmers. They depended on good weather and healthy crops for their survival. When harmful insect pests got into their crops, there was danger that they would not have enough food to survive. Middle Age farmers were always grateful when a group of colorful little beetles came along, because they knew the spotted beetles would eat the pests and save the crops.

Also at this time, many people worshipped Jesus, and they were grateful to him and to his mother, Mary, whom they called Our Lady. The people decided to name the little beetles in honor of Mary, and ever since they have been known as ladybugs.

Directions: How did you get your name? Talk to your parents or the person who gave you your name and find out why it was chosen. If you have a middle name, find out about it, too. In the space below, write your name and why it was chosen.

Your Name

Extra: If you had a ladybug for a pet, what would you call it? _____

Our Heroes

Orange tree growers in California have many reasons to be thankful for ladybugs. One of those reasons started many years ago. In the 1880's, a strange insect attacked the orange trees and began to damage them. The insects were called cottony-cushion scale insects. They came to California from Australia on a cargo ship, and right away they began to cause trouble.

The orange growers became worried. They did not know what to do about the cottony-cushion scale insects. Then they found out that the fruit growers in Australia were able to control the pests. Ladybugs naturally ate the pesky insects. The California growers ordered five hundred ladybugs to be sent to them. Those five hundred had many ladybug babies, and together they got the cottony-cushion scale insects under control. In two years, the orange trees were saved! The ladybugs became heroes to the California fruit farmers.

Directions: A hero is someone who solves a big problem by using his or her courage, intelligence, or strength. Do you know any heroes? Write the name of a hero you know and tell why that person is a hero.

My Hero

Ladybugs Are for Luck

For many hundreds of years, people have believed that ladybugs are lucky. Some people even believed that they have magical powers. In the lines below, you can read some beliefs people have had about ladybugs. Then be ready to write your thoughts about one of the beliefs.

Beliefs About Ladybugs

 If a ladybug walks across your hand, you will have good luck.

 If a ladybug is found in your house in the winter, you will have good luck.

  Ladybugs are a sign of good weather.

 When a farmer sees a ladybug, it means he or she will have good crops.

If a ladybug walks across a young woman's hand, she will be married within one year.

If a ladybug lands on a young woman's hand, she can say, "Fly away home," and then watch it fly away. Her future husband will come from wherever the ladybug goes.

   Ladybugs cure toothaches.

   Ladybugs cure colic.

   Ladybugs cure measles.

  Ladybugs are the companions of gnomes and fairies.

Ladybugs Are for Luck *(cont.)*

Directions: Choose one of the beliefs. Write a story about a ladybug and how it helps someone in the way it says in the belief. Draw a picture to go with your story.

36

Crossword

Directions: Use what you know about ladybugs to find the right answer for each clue. Fill in the answers on the crossword puzzle.

Across

2. This pest is a favorite food for ladybugs.
4. Ladybugs are part of this family.
7. Ladybugs help keep flowers in this place safe from insect pests.
9. Ladybugs have two sets of these.
10. This is what a ladybug is called in Great Britain.
11. These creatures have six legs and three body parts.
13. These cover the outer wings of many ladybugs.

Down

1. Ladybugs are not good fliers compared to some other bugs, so they prefer to do this.
3. This is what a ladybug does in the winter.
5. When a ladybug lays these, they are yellow.
6. This is the name for a ladybug grub after it comes out of its egg.
8. This is the special name for a ladybug's hard outer wings.
12. This is the number of legs a ladybug has.

Teacher Note: Fold the answer box under before duplicating to create a greater challenge for the children.

Answer Box				
aphid	elytra	insects	six	wings
beetle	garden	ladybird	spots	
eggs	hibernates	larva	walk	

Language Arts

Wordsearch

Directions: Find the ladybug words that are hidden in the word puzzle. The words are in the Word Box. Look for them across or down.

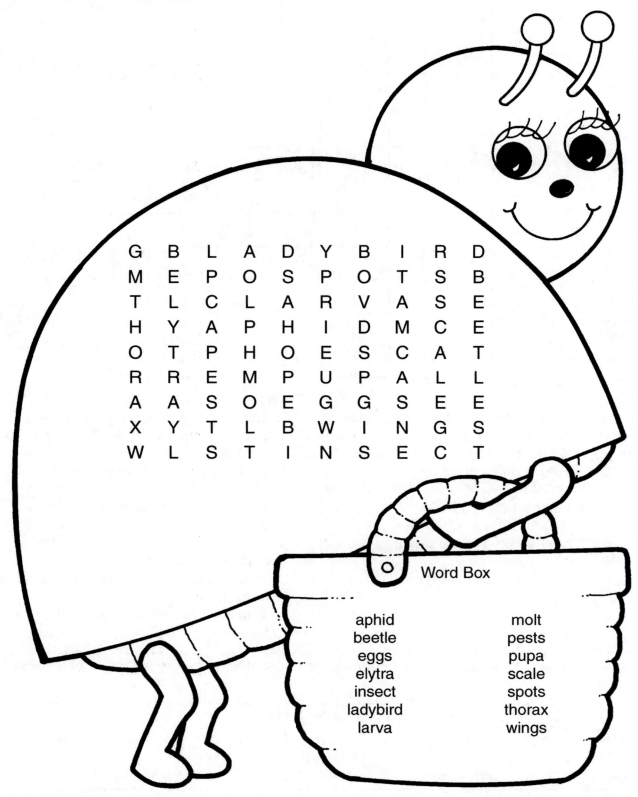

```
G  B  L  A  D  Y  B  I  R  D
M  E  P  O  S  P  O  T  S  B
T  L  C  L  A  R  V  A  S  E
H  Y  A  P  H  I  D  M  C  E
O  T  P  H  O  E  S  C  A  T
R  R  E  M  P  U  P  A  L  L
A  A  S  O  E  G  G  S  E  E
X  Y  T  L  B  W  I  N  G  S
W  L  S  T  I  N  S  E  C  T
```

Word Box

aphid   molt
beetle   pests
eggs   pupa
elytra   scale
insect   spots
ladybird   thorax
larva   wings

38 © Teacher Created Materials, Inc.

Ladybug Poetry

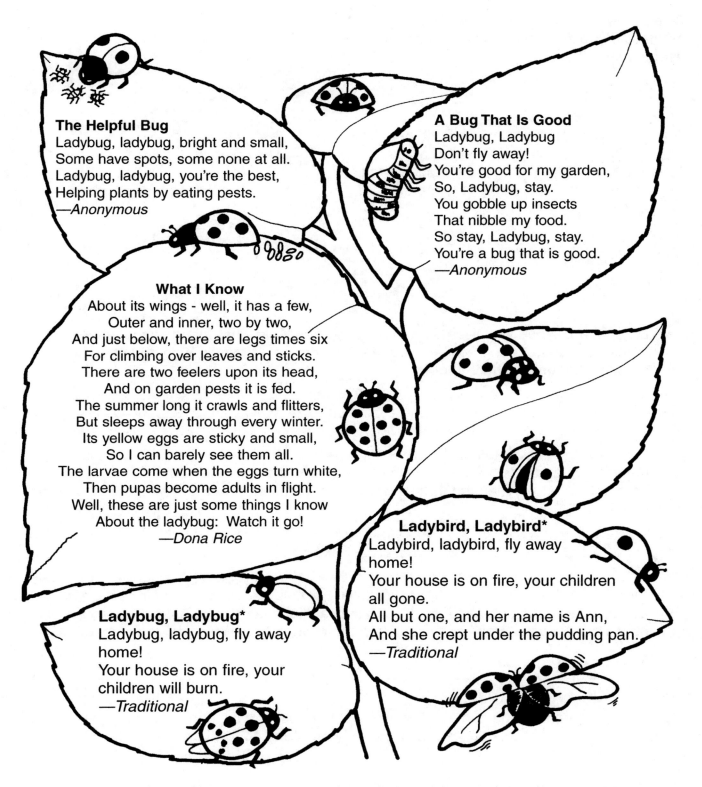

The Helpful Bug
Ladybug, ladybug, bright and small,
Some have spots, some none at all.
Ladybug, ladybug, you're the best,
Helping plants by eating pests.
—Anonymous

A Bug That Is Good
Ladybug, Ladybug
Don't fly away!
You're good for my garden,
So, Ladybug, stay.
You gobble up insects
That nibble my food.
So stay, Ladybug, stay.
You're a bug that is good.
—Anonymous

What I Know
About its wings - well, it has a few,
Outer and inner, two by two,
And just below, there are legs times six
For climbing over leaves and sticks.
There are two feelers upon its head,
And on garden pests it is fed.
The summer long it crawls and flitters,
But sleeps away through every winter.
Its yellow eggs are sticky and small,
So I can barely see them all.
The larvae come when the eggs turn white,
Then pupas become adults in flight.
Well, these are just some things I know
About the ladybug: Watch it go!
—Dona Rice

Ladybird, Ladybird*
Ladybird, ladybird, fly away home!
Your house is on fire, your children all gone.
All but one, and her name is Ann,
And she crept under the pudding pan.
—Traditional

Ladybug, Ladybug*
Ladybug, ladybug, fly away home!
Your house is on fire, your children will burn.
—Traditional

*These two rhymes come from times long ago when farmers burned their fields to clear away dead leaves and vines. Since ladybugs lived on these vines, their homes were burned, and since ladybug children cannot fly, they may have burned as well.

How Many?

Directions: Read the questions. Then write the math facts and solve the problems. The first has been done for you.

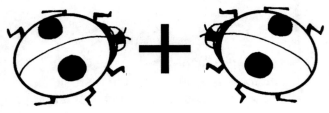

1. A ladybug named Larry was out for a walk when he met his good friend, Lonnie, another ladybug. Larry and Lonnie each have 6 legs. How many legs are there in all?

$$6 + 6 = 12$$

2. Lynette, a ladybug who lives on a rose bush, likes to visit her friend Lance, a ladybug on a nearby orange tree. Each ladybug has 2 antennae. When they get together, how many antennae are there in all?

3. Lilly Ladybug is a beautiful flier. She spreads her 2 inner wings beneath her 2 spotted outer wings and flitters from vine to vine. When she stops to rest, she meets Lola and Loretta Ladybug. When the three ladybugs get together, how many wings do they have in all?

4. Lucy Ladybug is going on a trip to visit Lyle and Lulu Ladybug and their new larva, Louise. Lucy Ladybug has 2 spots on her beautiful outer wings. Lyle, Lulu, and Louise each have 3 spots. How many spots are there when the four ladybugs get together?

5. A ladybug named Lou can eat 7 aphids each hour. His wife, Lana, can eat 5. Their two children, Lucky and Lupe, can each eat 3. How many aphids can the family of four eat in one hour?

From Least to Most

Directions: Cut out the ladybugs. Count their spots. Glue them to the next page in order from least to most.

From Least to Most (cont.)

Least

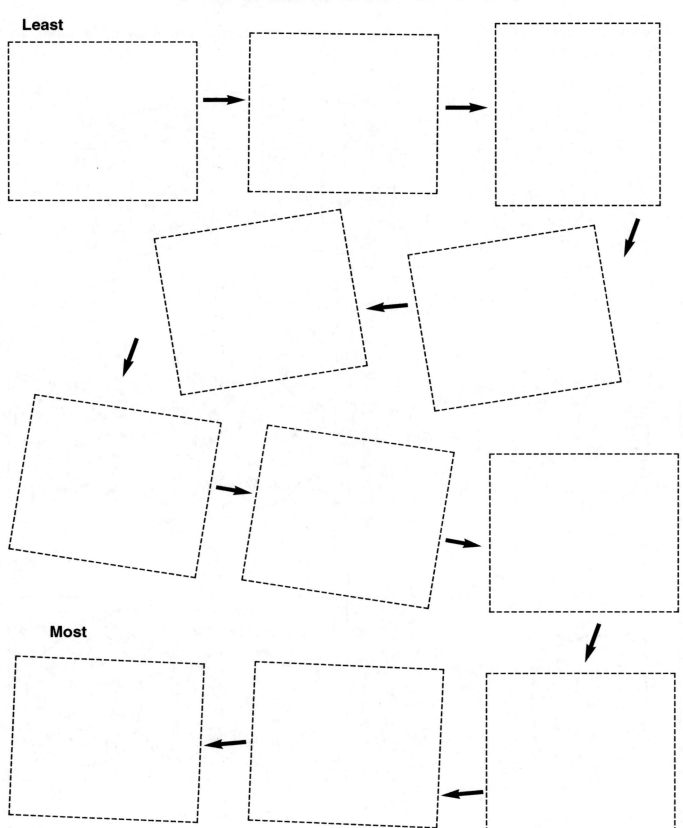

Most

Twenty

Directions: Follow all of the leaves that when added up equal 20 to get the ladybug home to its friends.

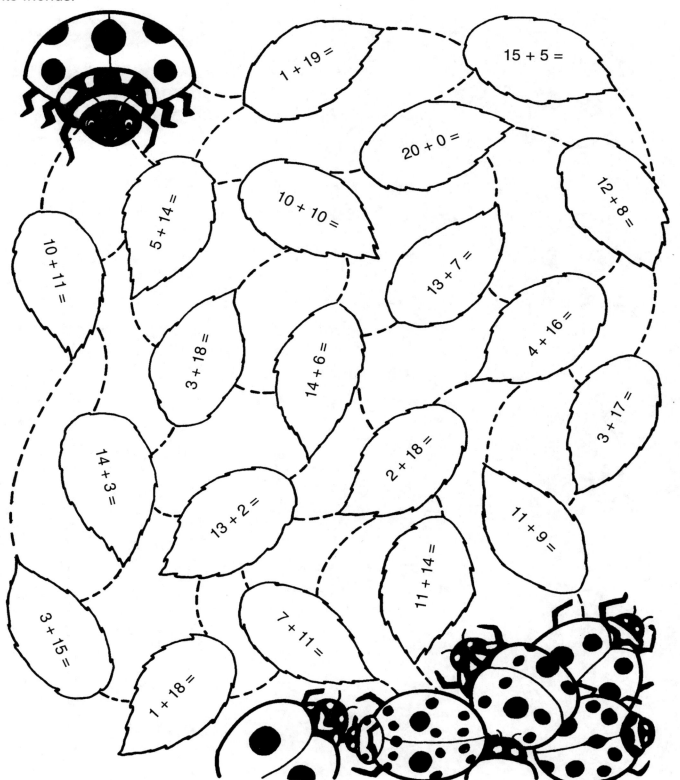

Name the Shape

Directions: Draw lines to match the shape names to the ladybugs with the shape spots.

1.
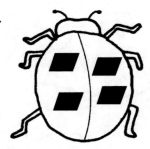

2.

rectangle

diamond

3.

circle

4.

square

5.

rhombus

6.

triangle

7.

oval

8.

octagon

Ladybug Symmetry

Directions: The spots on a ladybug's wings are symmetrical. That means that each wing matches the other. Draw spots on each empty wing, matching it to its partner. *Remember, the spots should be in the same position and the same size.* When you have finished drawing, color the ladybug.

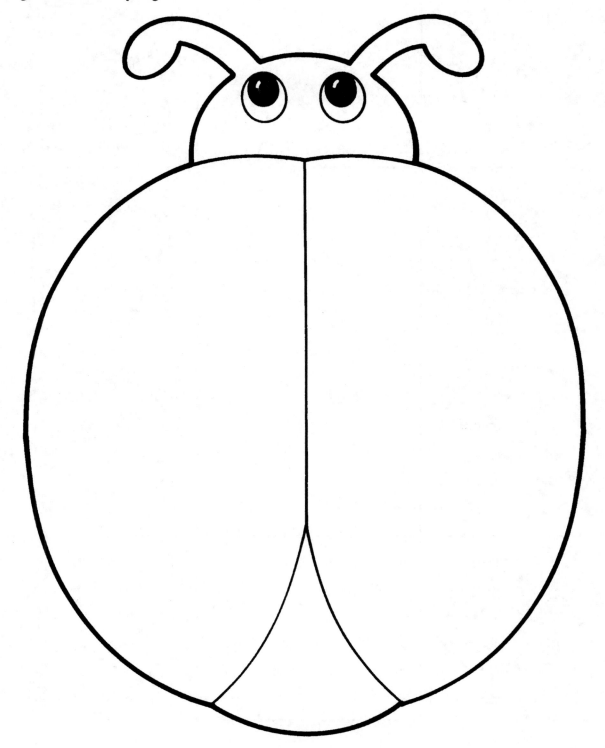

Match the Spots

Directions: Cut out the ladybugs on the dotted lines. Glue each ladybug next to its partner with the same number of spots.

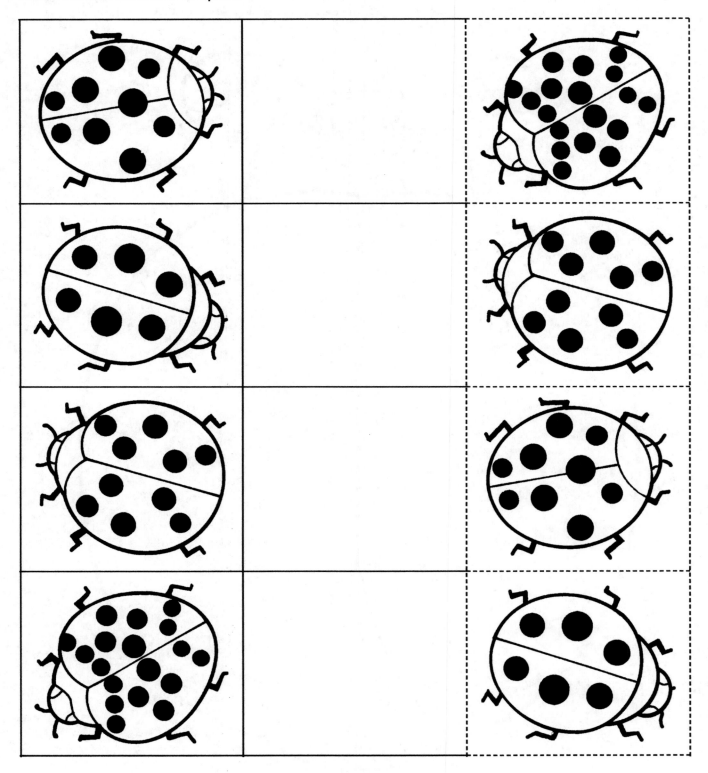

The Ladybug Game

Directions: Cut out the gameboard and sheet of task cards (page 48), glue them to the tagboard, and laminate. Cut around the cards to separate them. Provide a marker for each player and one die. To play, one player at a time chooses a task card and answers the question. If correct, the player rolls the die and moves that number of spaces. If incorrect, the player does not move. Play continues until one player reaches the finish. (**Tip:** To make the game self-checking, write an answer sheet on a separate piece of paper. To increase the skill, create more challenging task cards.)

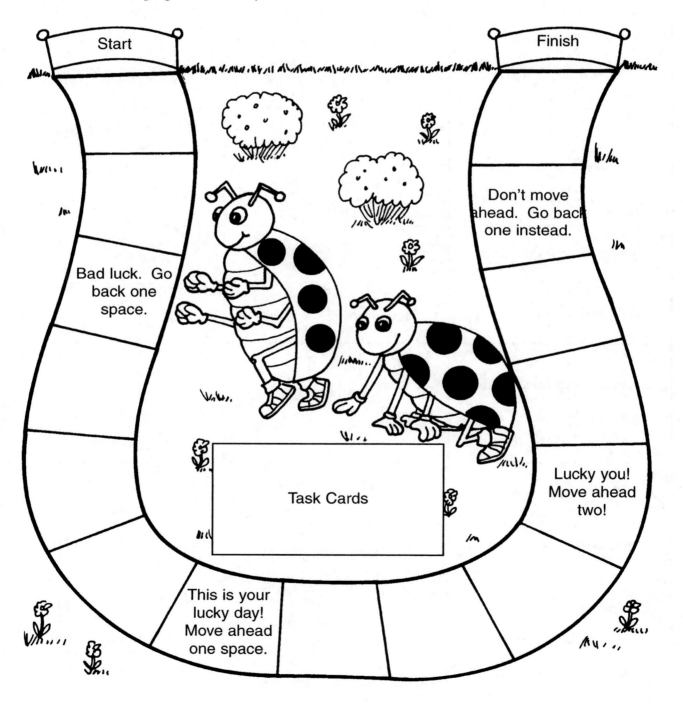

Start

Finish

Don't move ahead. Go back one instead.

Bad luck. Go back one space.

Task Cards

Lucky you! Move ahead two!

This is your lucky day! Move ahead one space.

The Ladybug Game *(cont.)*

1. 14 🐞s on a leaf 6 fly away How many 🐞s are left?	**2.** 5 🐞s and 2 🐞s meet 6 🐞s How many altogether?	**3.** 16 🐞s 7 🐞s more How many 🐞s in all?
4. 4 🐞s 4 leaves How many leaves for each 🐞?	**5.** 7 🐞s 11 more 🐞s How many 🐞s in all?	**6.** 5 pine cones 2 🐞s in each pine cone How many 🐞s in all?
7. 20 🐞s 16 fly to find some aphids How many 🐞s are left?	**8.** 3 🐞s 6 aphids How many aphids for each 🐞?	**9.** 3 🐞s and 4 🐞s meet 5 🐞s How many 🐞s in all?
10. 3 🐞 moms each have 10 🐞 eggs How many 🐞 eggs in all?	**11.** 11 🐞 boys 13 🐞 girls How many 🐞s in all?	**12.** 18 🐞s find 14 aphids How many more 🐞s than aphids?
13. 3 leaves each have 5 🐞s How many 🐞s in all?	**14.** 14 🐞s 6 🐞s find food How many 🐞s did not find food?	**15.** 1 mother 🐞 1 father 🐞 16 🐞 larvae How many in the 🐞 family?
16. 7 🐞s and 2 🐞s meet 9 🐞s How many 🐞s in all?	**17.** 13 🐞s on a vine 9 🐞s fly away How many 🐞s are left?	**18.** 7 🐞s 14 aphids How many aphids for each 🐞?
19. 6 🐞s on a rose bush 8 more 🐞s come How many 🐞s in all?	**20.** 1 mother 🐞 1 father 🐞 21 🐞 larvae How many in the 🐞 family?	**21.** 17 🐞s in the air 10 🐞s on a vine How many 🐞s in all?

All Kinds of Ladybugs

Directions: There are more than 4,000 kinds of ladybugs. On this page, you will name five of the most common types. To do it, look at the code. Then solve the problems, using the code to write the correct letters in the blanks. What are the five kinds of ladybugs?

1. ___ ___ ___   –   ___ ___ ___ ___ ___ ___ ___
    5+15 16+7 9+6   7+12 4+12 8+7 10+10 2+18 3+2 1+3

    ladybug

2. ___ ___ ___ ___   ___ ___ ___ ___
    1+0 11+8 4+4 5+20   3+4 9+9 0+1 12+13

    ladybug

3. ___ ___ ___ ___   –   ___ ___ ___ ___ ___ ___ ___
    7+7 3+6 11+3 5+0   1+18 10+6 6+9 0+20 17+3 1+4 2+2

    ladybug

4. ___ ___ ___ ___ ___ ___ ___ ___
    3+16 4+12 14+1 17+3 4+8 2+3 4+15 9+10

    ladybug

5. ___ ___ ___ ___ ___ ___ ___ ___ ___ ___
    1+2 7+8 2+12 11+11 4+1 4+14 5+2 2+3 8+6 7+13

    ladybug

A	B	C	D	E	F	G	H	I	J	K	L	M
1	2	3	4	5	6	7	8	9	10	11	12	13

N	O	P	Q	R	S	T	U	V	W	X	Y	Z
14	15	16	17	18	19	20	21	22	23	24	25	26

Ladybug Pencil Poke

Directions: Color, cut out, and laminate the ladybug shape. Punch holes along the perimeter of the ladybug. Staple two craft sticks to the bottom of the ladybug, placing one on each side of the bug, to use as a handle. Using erasable marker, write an operation sign (+, −, x, ÷, =) in the center circle. Write a different problem next to each hole you punched. On the reverse, write the answer to each problem next to the corresponding hole.

To use the pencil poke, one child faces the ladybug while another holds it from behind. The child facing it pokes a pencil through any hole and says the problem aloud, giving the answer. The child in back checks the answer. When all the problems have been answered, the children switch places.

You can change the function of the pencil poke by wiping away the problems and answers and writing in new ones. You can even let each child create a pencil poke of his or her own to challenge one another.

Open Worksheet

Directions: Cut out and glue the ladybug spots on the next page to the spots below, matching the answers to the problems.

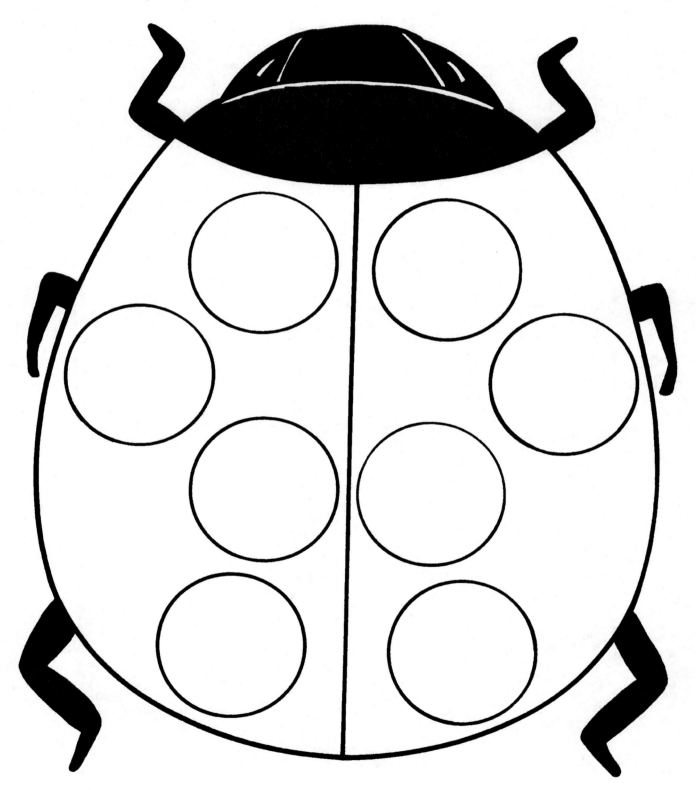

Open Worksheet *(cont.)*

See page 51 for directions.

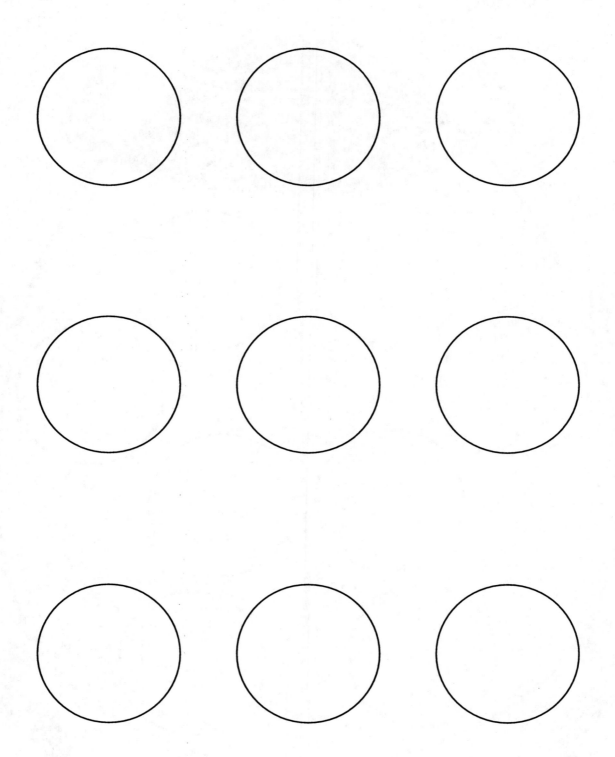

Follow That Bug!

Directions: Look at the map of the garden. Follow the directions below.

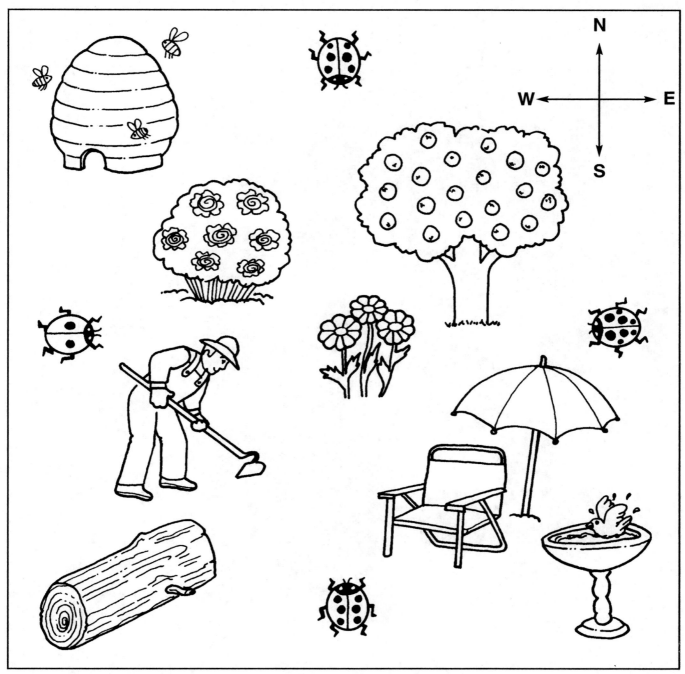

1. Draw a red path from the north ladybug to the rose bush.
2. Draw a yellow path from the west ladybug to the daisies.
3. Draw an orange path from east ladybug to the orange tree.
4. Draw a green path from the south ladybug to the lawn chair.
5. Color the object in the southwest corner brown. This is where the ladybugs will spend the winter.

Be an Entomologist

Direction: An entomologist studies insects. Be an entomologist by labeling the ladybug parts.

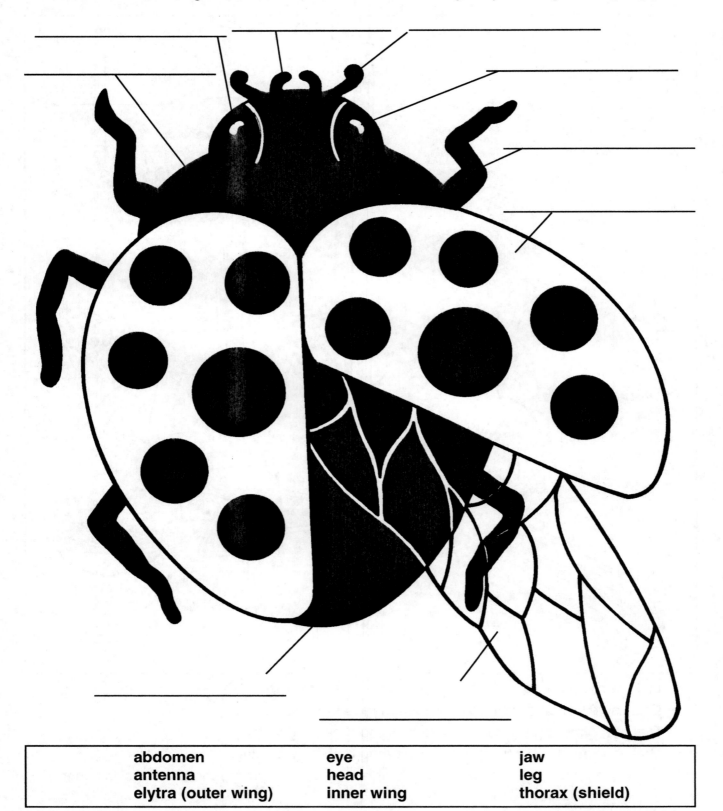

abdomen	eye	jaw
antenna	head	leg
elytra (outer wing)	inner wing	thorax (shield)

Food Chain

There is a normal cycle of life for every creature on the planet. Some lives are usually very short while others are often very long. There are many factors that go into the relative lengths of lives, but one important factor is where each creature sits on the planetary food chain.

Share with the children that the life cycles of some animals come to an end because the animal gets old and dies. Other animals die because they are the prey (food) of other animal predators (hunters). Even though this may seem sad to the children, it is good for them to know that the cycle of predator/prey in the world is an important way for nature to keep the planet healthy with everything in balance. If there were too many of one kind of animal on the earth, they would take up space and resources needed by other kinds. Of course, too many animals altogether would take up space needed by humans. Also, people are grateful that some creatures (such as insect pests) are the prey of others because these pests can destroy plants that are important food sources for people.

Let the children know that many of the animals that become prey are the weak, sick, or old. They are also usually smaller animals than the predators. The pattern of larger animal predators eating smaller animal prey is called the "food chain." The food chain tells an eating "story." For example, when asked, "What eats aphids?" the children will answer, "Ladybugs eat aphids." They know that ladybugs are bigger than aphids. When asked, "What eats ladybugs?" the children know it is something larger than ladybugs, such as a robin or other small bird. In turn, the robin is eaten by several different four-legged animals, such as a fox, which is bigger than a robin.

To illustrate the food chain, let the children complete the activity on the next page. When finished, discuss how the body of the fox, when dead, will decay and become a part of the earth. In the earth, it will nourish plants. The plants will nourish the aphids, and the aphids will nourish the ladybugs, and so on. It is the "circle of life."

Extension: As a class, watch the animated film, *The Lion King* (Walt Disney Productions, 1994). Pay careful attention to the circle-of-life theme that is interwoven throughout the movie. The story stresses the importance in nature of everything taking its rightful place so that all of nature prospers. In the film, we see how disorder leads to the ruin of natural resources and threatens the livelihood of every living thing.

When you finish watching the film, brainstorm as a class for ways in which you can help to maintain the orderly balance of nature. Discuss such concepts as recycling and conservation. Plan a way the class can work together throughout the school year to help the planet. Help the children uncover ways they can help the planet on their own as well.

Food Chain *(cont.)*

Directions: Color the animal strips. Cut them out. Glue or tape the aphids strip to make the first chain link. Loop the ladybug strip through the aphids strip, showing that the ladybugs "eat" the aphids. Tape or glue the ladybugs strip, making the second link. Next, add the robin strip and then finally the fox, showing that the robin eats the ladybugs and the fox eats the robin.

Fox

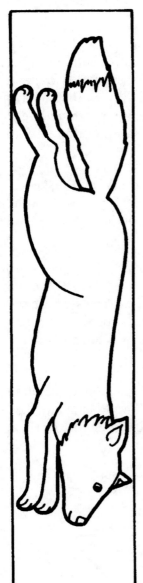

Robin

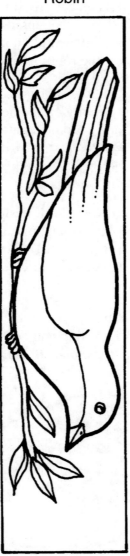

Ladybugs

Aphids

Observing Ladybugs

This experience will take some pre-planning. Begin by purchasing live ladybugs. You will then create a Ladybug Viewing Center.

Supplies

- 50-100 ladybugs*
- cottonball soaked in water (change it every day)
- clusters of live aphids on stalks cut from rosebushes (periodically provide fresh stalks)

Note: If rosebushes are unavailable, cut raisins into fourths and provide them as imitation aphids.

- bits of grass
- cheesecloth
- large rubberband
- clear plastic container with no lid (food storage types work well)

Directions

1. Lay the grass, cottonball, and aphid stalks into the bottom of the container.
2. Add the ladybugs.
3. Cover the container with cheesecloth, secured with the rubberband.
4. Create a viewing center by placing the ladybug container on a table or counter with magnifying glasses, data-capture sheets, pencils, and crayons.
5. Encourage the children to observe the ladybugs and aphids daily, drawing pictures on the data-capture sheets of what they see.
6. After a week of observation, gather the children to discuss their findings. Ask them what the ladybugs eat, how they eat, and other pertinent questions. Allow them to share what they have observed.

*To purchase live ladybugs, you can go to a local garden center. You can also order them through *Insect Lore*, a catalog company that offers science and nature products, including live bugs. See the bibliography on page 79 for information on how to contact *Insect Lore*. (Please be aware that ladybugs are available July through March only.)

Observing Ladybugs:
Data-Capture Sheet

Directions: Draw a picture of ladybugs or aphids as you see them under a magnifying glass.

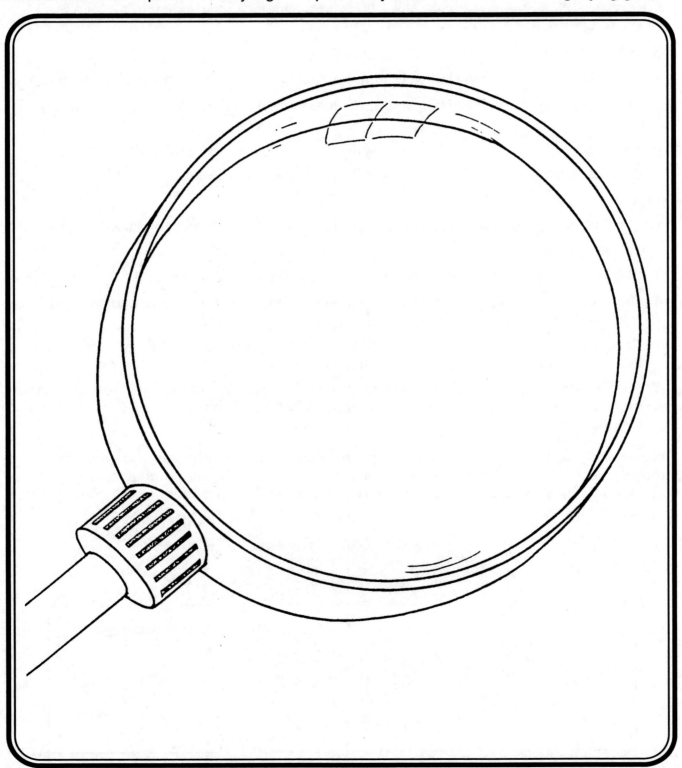

58

Life Cycle 2

The following activity creates a three-dimensional life cycle wheel for ladybugs.

Materials Per Child:

- 9" (23 cm) white paper plate, divided into four quarters with marker
- 4 green construction paper leaves, approximately 2" x 3" (5 cm x 7.5 cm)
- 3 red buttons (1" / 2.5 cm) (Add "heads" and "spots" with black tempera paint.)
- 1 orange button ($^5/_8$" / 1.5 cm) (Add black paint for head area only.)
- 4 yellow pompons (3 mm)
- tiny handful of dry white or wild rice
- 3 pieces of black chenille stick ($^1/_4$" / .5 cm)
- 2 twigs (1.5" / 4 cm)
- white styrofoam packaging "peanut"
- sheet of fact boxes (page 60)
- pencil
- scissors
- glue
- black and orange markers

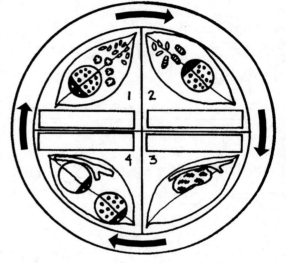

Directions:

1. Label each section of the paper plate (clockwise from the top left) 1, 2, 3, and 4.

2. Glue one green leaf in each section.

3. Glue ten grains of rice (aphids) on the corner of leaf #1. Glue one red ladybug button near the center of the same leaf with its head facing away from the aphids. Glue four yellow pompons (eggs) near the tail end of the ladybug. Cut out and glue fact box #1 under the leaf.

4. Glue four grains of rice in the matching corner area of leaf #2. Glue a ladybug button onto the leaf with its head facing the aphids. Between the ladybug and the aphids, glue three pieces of chenille stick (larvae). Cut out and glue fact box #2 under the leaf.

5. Glue one twig near the top edge of green leaf #3. Glue the styrofoam peanut (pupa) next to (as if clinging to) the twig. For added detail, dab bits of orange and black marker on the pupa to give it realistic color. Cut out and glue fact box #3 over the leaf.

6. Glue the second twig near the top edge of green leaf #4. Glue the orange button ladybug next to the twig, as if it just hatched from the pupa. Glue the remaining red ladybug near the bottom of the green leaf. Cut out and glue fact box #4 over the leaf.

7. Draw an arrow from section #1 to section #2, section #2 to section #3, and so on, showing the life cycle progression.

Life Cycle 2: Fact Boxes

1 The ladybug lays eggs on a green leaf near aphids.	**2** The eggs hatch. The black baby ladybugs (larvae) eat the aphids.
3 After a larva grows, its skin forms a pupa to hide in and change.	**4** When the grown-up ladybug comes out of the pupa, it is orange. By the next day, it will turn red and black.

1 The ladybug lays eggs on a green leaf near aphids.	**2** The eggs hatch. The black baby ladybugs (larvae) eat the aphids.
3 After a larva grows, its skin forms a pupa to hide in and change.	**4** When the grown-up ladybug comes out of the pupa, it is orange. By the next day, it will turn red and black.

1 The ladybug lays eggs on a green leaf near aphids.	**2** The eggs hatch. The black baby ladybugs (larvae) eat the aphids.
3 After a larva grows, its skin forms a pupa to hide in and change.	**4** When the grown-up ladybug comes out of the pupa, it is orange. By the next day, it will turn red and black.

Insects?

Most young children think that all bugs are insects. This experiment will help them to realize that this is not true. They will start to appreciate the details that help us to differentiate between bugs and insects.

Materials

- 8–12 plastic bugs
- index cards
- black marker
- glue or two-sided tape
- Lab Worksheet 1 or 2 (see pages 62–63)

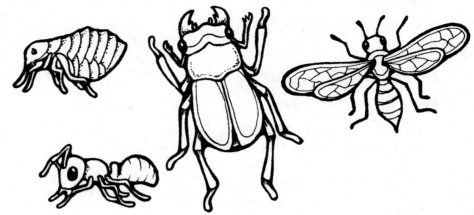

Directions

1. Collect the plastic bugs wherever available. Some places to look include novelty shops, nature stores, and the little trinket machines near the entrance to many grocery stores. Some children may own the toy that makes "bugs" by cooking liquid plastic. If so, they may be willing to make some bugs for the class.

2. Affix each bug to an index card, using glue or two-sided tape. Write a letter of the alphabet on the card, using a different letter for each bug.

3. Discuss or review with the children the characteristics of insects: six legs, exoskeleton, and three body segments. Also discuss the characteristics of other closely related animals such as spiders, ticks, and centipedes. Talk about the differences between what we commonly refer to as bugs (any wingless or four-winged insect; mouthparts used for piercing and sucking) and insects (usually small invertebrates with an exoskeleton; adults have six legs, three body segments, and two pairs of wings).

4. Talk about how to classify animals. Ask children what types of characteristics they can use to classify animals. Brainstorm a list of characteristics.

5. Discuss how to enter data in a table. Then let the children complete either Lab Worksheet 1 or 2, depending on their level. Worksheet 2 requires a slightly elevated cognitive skill.

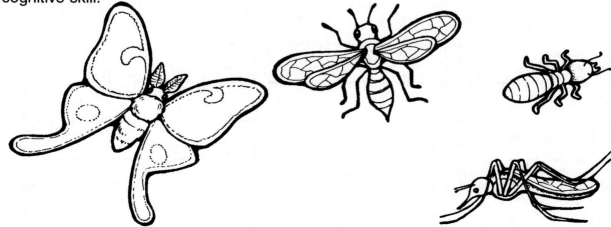

Lab Worksheet 1

Question Are all bugs insects?

What You Need

- 1 set of bugs (can be plastic or real)

What You Do

1. Count the legs on each bug.
2. Write the number of legs on each bug in the table below.
3. Put an X under Yes if you think the bug is an insect. Put an X under No if you do not think the bug is an insect.

Bug	Number of Legs	Is this an insect?	
		Yes	**No**
A			
B			
C			
D			
E			
F			
G			
H			
I			
J			
K			
L			

What You Learned: Are all bugs insects? _____ Yes _____ No (Check one.)

Lab Worksheet 2

Question: How can you tell if a bug is an insect or not?

What You Need
- 1 set of bugs (can be plastic or real)

What You Do
1. Look at each bug.
2. Fill out the table below to tell about each bug.

Bug	Is this an insect?		Why or why not?
	Yes	**No**	
A			
B			
C			
D			
E			
F			
G			
H			
I			
J			
K			
L			

What You Learned:

How can you tell if a bug is an insect or not? _____

Thumbprint Art

Directions: Press your thumb on an inkpad and then make thumbprints all over this scene. Add details to your thumbprints to turn them into ladybugs!

This and That

There are a number of simple ladybug art projects that you and your children can make. Here are a few of them.

Magnets and Pins

Materials

- red pompons
- black felt
- hole punch
- craft glue
- safety pin or magnet
- glue gun (for adult use only)

Directions

1. Give each child a pompon and some black felt. Let them use the hole punch to make black spots for the ladybug from the felt. Glue the spots on to the pompon with the craft glue.

2. Using a hot glue gun, attach a magnet or safety pin to the bottom of the ladybug. (Only an adult should handle the glue gun.) Let the glue harden before returning the magnet or pin to the child.

Clip

Materials

- red pompons
- black felt
- hole punch
- craft glue
- clothespins

Directions

1. Decorate the pompon with felt spots, as above.

2. Glue a ladybug pompon to the end of a clothespin; allow the glue to dry.

3. Use the ladybug clips in the classroom to hold or hang papers, or have the children take them home as gifts for their parents.

Crayon Relief

Materials

- drawing paper
- white crayons
- watercolor paints
- paintbrushes

Directions

1. Instruct each child to draw a nature scene with ladybugs, using white crayon. They should only draw the outlines of the shapes. A good idea for a nature scene would be a flower bush with ladybugs.

2. Let each child go over the scene with watercolor paints, either in stripes of color across the page or different colors painted lightly over each object.

3. Allow to dry and then display the crayon reliefs around the room. An added touch would be to hang them on a line using your ladybug clips!

Ladybug Games

These three pages suggest a variety of ways you can bring the ladybug theme into your movement or physical education activities.

Ladybug Life Cycle Lines

Materials:

- large, open space (inside or outside)
- masking tape

Directions:

1. Place long strips of masking tape on the ground surface as starting line A. Approximately 30 yards (25 meters) away, place parallel masking tape strips on the ground surface as starting line B.

2. Divide the class in half to form two teams. Divide the teams in half again, placing half of the team members behind starting lines A and B (facing each other in relay-race style).

3. When given the signal to begin, the first child behind line A hops-squats-hops-squats to line B (ladybug laying eggs on a leaf) and touches the hand of team member B. Team member B crawls on the ground surface on all fours back to line A (ladybug baby going toward an aphid meal) and touches the next team member A. This team member somersaults or hops back to line B (ladybug in pupa stage) and touches the next team member B. This team member runs with arms extended (flying adult ladybug) back to line A, and the cycle begins again until all team members have participated. (Note: This can be a true relay race or just done for fun.)

Ladybug Facts

Materials:

- Fact or False? cards (page 68)
- large, open space (inside or outside)

Directions:

1. Duplicate and cut apart the cards on the page 68.
2. Let the children spread out across the open area.
3. Read a card. (Do not read the word "true" or "false." Let the children determine for themselves.) If the statement is a fact, the children should run around with their arms outstretched (like a ladybug in flight). If it is false, they should crawl around on all fours (like a ladybug walking).

To make a competition of the facts, have the children who walk when they should crawl (or vice versa) leave the playing field area. The last ladybug on the field wins.

Ladybug Games *(cont.)*

Ladybug, May I?

Materials:

- large, open space (inside or outside)

Directions:

1. Play the game Mother, May I?, but use "Ladybug" in place of "Mother." To play, one child is the "ladybug." He or she stands at a distance across from the other children. The rest of the class stands in a row, side by side. The ladybug calls the name of one child and says, for example, "Brian, you may take three hops." Brian must respond, "Ladybug, may I?" to which the ladybug says, "Yes." If Brian does not ask the question or wait for the answer before moving, he cannot take the hops.

2. Use special commands that a ladybug would do such as crawl, fly, or roll over. Make up other commands as well. For example, a "pupal roll" could be a somersault and a "larva leap" could be a giant step.

Food Chain Freeze Tag

Materials:

- large, open space (inside or outside)
- straight or safety pins (two per child)
- 9" x 12" (23 cm x 30 cm) construction paper (green, red, orange, and brown)

Directions:

1. Divide the class as evenly as possible into four groups. Each group represents animals in the food chain: aphids (green construction paper), ladybugs (red construction paper), robins (orange construction paper), and foxes (brown construction paper).

2. Cut each piece of construction paper in half. Pin half to the front of each child's clothing and half to the back for easy identification. Review the food chain concept and which animal (color) eats which other animal (color). (A good pre-activity is completing page 56.)

3. Have the children spread out over a large space in random order. When given a signal, each animal chases after its prey and tries to "eat" it (tagged by tapping gently with one hand). If touched, the animal is "eaten" and must "freeze." (For very young children, you may wish to prepare a piece of chart paper, displaying construction paper color sheets and arrows identifying who may touch [eat] whom.)

4. To extend the activity with the circle-of-life concept, instruct the "aphids" to chase the "foxes." Explain to the children that when the foxes die, their bodies decay and nourish the earth. The earth nourishes the plants, and the plants nourish the aphids. Therefore, the circle is complete.

Ladybug Games *(cont.)*

See page 66 for suggested use.

True or False? Cards

True: Ladybugs are beetles.	**True:** Ladybugs lay 10 to 100 eggs at one time.	**False:** Ladybugs have one pair of wings.
True: Ladybugs are insects.	**True:** Ladybugs lay their eggs on leaves that have plenty of aphids on them.	**False:** Ladybugs eat other helpful bugs.
True: There are male and female ladybugs.	**True:** Ladybug eggs are sticky and yellow.	**False:** Ladybugs are only red and black.
True: Ladybugs have three main body parts.	**True:** Ladybugs go through metamorphosis.	**False:** Ladybugs lay one egg at a time.
True: Ladybugs have six legs.	**True:** New ladybugs have no spots.	**False:** Ladybugs lay their eggs in nests.
True: Ladybugs use their legs for walking, climbing, and cleaning themselves.	**True:** Some adult ladybugs have no spots.	**False:** Ladybug eggs are blue with hard shells.
True: Ladybugs have two sets of wings.	**True:** Ladybugs hibernate during the winter.	**False:** Ladybugs look the same when they are born as they do when they are adults.
True: Ladybugs eat harmful insect pests.	**False:** Ladybugs are all females.	**False:** All ladybugs have spots.
True: Ladybugs come in many colors.	**False:** Ladybugs have eight legs.	**False:** Ladybugs are born with spots.
True: Ladybugs can eat up to 100 aphids in one day.	**False:** Ladybugs use their legs for spinning webs.	**False:** Ladybugs sleep through the summer.

68

"Aphid"tizing Snacks

Here are two fun and simple ways to make delicious ladybug snacks.

A Ladybug A Day

Supplies

- plastic knives
- sharp knife (adult use only)

Ingredients

- red apples
- peanut butter
- raisins

Preparation

1. Cut the apples in half. Cut each half in half again.
2. Give each child two pieces.
3. Let the children stick their two apple pieces together with peanut butter. These will make the ladybug's wings.
4. Cut the raisins in half. Give each child several halves.
5. Have the children put spots on the apple wings by sticking dabs of peanut butter to the raisin halves and sticking the raisins onto the apple wings.
6. Admire the ladybugs—and eat away!

Ladybug Freeze

Supplies

- rounded ice cream scoop
- sturdy paper plates
- plastic spoons

Ingredients

- strawberry ice cream
- chocolate chips
- black licorice shoestring vines

Preparation

1. Cut the licorice into 1" (2.5 cm) pieces. Give each child two pieces.
2. Cut additional licorice into pieces about 4" to 5" (10 cm to 12.5 cm) long. Give each child one.
3. Give each child 12–16 chocolate chips.
4. Scoop the ice cream into balls. Give each child a scoop of the ice cream on a plate.
5. Let the children decorate their ladybugs by laying the long strip of licorice down the middle of the ice cream to create ladybug wings. Then insert the two short pieces of licorice at the head to make the antennae. Finally, the chocolate chips can be used to make spots by inserting them in the ice cream wing areas, pointed down.
6. Eat and enjoy!

Ladybug Cake

This cake will take a bit of work, but the children will love the results!

Supplies

- 1.5 quart (1.3 liter) oven-proof bowl
- mixer
- mixing bowl
- knife
- long toothpick
- cooling rack
- cardboard
- aluminum foil
- waxed paper
- scissors
- jellyroll pan or cookie sheet
- double boiler
- stirring spoon
- oven and stove

Ingredients

- 1 package poundcake mix (16 oz./500 g)
- 2 cans white frosting and 1 can dark chocolate frosting (16 oz./500 g each)
- red paste food coloring
- black licorice shoestring vines
- black licorice coins
- 2 white candy wafers
- 2 black candy gumdrops
- 1 red fruit chew candy
- 2 Scooter® pies

Preparation

1. Mix the poundcake according to the box directions. Pour it into the oven-proof bowl and bake for 50-60 minutes or until the toothpick inserted in the cake comes out clean.
2. Cool on a rack for 10 minutes. Remove from the bowl and cool completely.
3. Cut out a cardboard circle (the diameter of the cake) and cover it with foil.
4. Cut a slice from one side of the cake, leaving exposed a section about 2.5" (7 cm) square.
5. Place the cake on the cardboard, and transfer it back to the cooling rack.
6. Line the jellyroll pan or cookie sheet with waxed paper and place the cooling rack with cake over the paper.
7. Put the white frosting in the top of the double boiler and add red coloring. Heat it over simmering water, stirring occasionally. When the frosting is the consistency of heavy cream (about 5 minutes), pour it slowly over the cake. Reheat the frosting that has landed on the jellyroll pan or cookie sheet as necessary so that the frosting eventually covers the entire cake (except cut flat area). Let the cake and frosting stand for a few minutes to set.
8. Press a strip of licorice down the middle of the cake to make the ladybug's wings. Press the licorice coins into the wings to make the spots. Let cake and frosting stand until dry.
9. Cut .5'' (1.25 cm) from one circular end of each Scooter® pie. Attach the pies with chocolate frosting, and cut across the bottom to make them flat. This will be the ladybug's head.
10. Spread some chocolate frosting over the exposed part of the cake. Attach the ladybug head and cover it entirely with frosting.
11. Press on white candies for eyes. Attach the gumdrops with frosting to the eyes to make pupils. Cut the fruit chew in half. Roll half into a ball to make a nose. Place it on the head. Shape the other half into a mouth and attach it. Cut two strips of licorice and attach them to the top of the head for feelers. If desired, use licorice to make eyelashes, as well.

       70

Have a Ball!

It is always a pleasure to have a party when culminating a unit, but here is a special party idea that will involve the creativity and cooperation of all the children. Begin by gathering the work completed throughout the unit and displaying it around the classroom. Talk about the beauty of ladybugs and how they are well-loved the world over. Also discuss the fact that many insects and other crawling and flying creatures are not so well liked. Brainstorm lists of those bugs people generally like and those bugs people generally do not like. Let the children share about their own bug interests and prejudices. Then prepare for and host a "Beautiful Bug Ball!"

In 1963, Disney animators created a cartoon (*Summer Magic*) that used a song called "The Ugly Bug Ball," written by Richard M. and Robert B. Sherman. The song is sung by Burl Ives. Today, the song can be found on a Disney collection tape or compact disc called *Classic Disney: Volume 1* (The Walt Disney Company, 1995). The song is delightful. It tells the story of a caterpillar who turns to his beetle (ladybug) friend, bemoaning his lonely lot in life. The beetle tells the caterpillar about "the annual ugly bug ball" where the caterpillar can meet many new friends. The caterpillar joins spiders, crickets, ants, fleas, and more at the ball, and there he finds his future bride. The chorus of the song is particularly catching, and the music itself is playful and rollicking. The story virtually calls out to be told. Your children are sure to enjoy the music as well as the story. (*Please note: For your culminating activity, refer to the ball as a beautiful, not ugly ball.*)

Play the song for the children and let them learn the lyrics. Then, as a class, prepare either a musical skit (with costumes) or a puppet show incorporating the band of characters from the song. (The named characters include a male and female caterpillar, a ladybird beetle, a spider, a dragonfly, crickets, ants, fleas, and worms.) Learn the song, and on your party date, perform the musical skit or puppet show for parents or other classrooms. (Pay close attention to the use of horns in the song: they will make a great addition to any show.) Let the ladybird beetle (ladybug) introduce the play and choreograph the bugs at the ball. There are musical interludes between the verses and will be great opportunities for some fancy steps. Offer programs to your guests which have been printed on the ladybug stationery (page 77). Include each child's name on the program for a special keepsake.

After the show, invite your guests to tour around your classroom, observing the many things your class has accomplished throughout the unit. Complete the party by eating the ladybug cake (page 70) and serving it along with some red punch. If desired, offer each guest a child-made keepsake such as the ladybug magnet or pin (page 65).

Have a Ball! *(cont.)*

You are cordially invited
to attend the

Beautiful Bug Ball!

Hosted by our beautiful
friends

The Ladybugs

and lots of other special
creatures.

Where: _____

When: _____

Time: _____

Letter to Parents

Duplicate the letter below, filling in the information that pertains to your needs.

Dear Parents,

Did you know that ladybugs are really called ladybird beetles? That is just one of the many things we will learn in our upcoming unit on ladybugs. It is an exciting unit, rich with activities in all subject areas. We are going to be very busy, but in order to make our learning the best possible, we are asking for your help. We will need the following supplies to complete our unit:

_____   _____

_____   _____

_____   _____

_____   _____

If you can donate any of these supplies, please send them by _____.

We can also use your help in the classroom. If you can help during any of the times listed below, circle them and return the bottom portion of this letter by _____.

Thanks!

_____

Yes, I can help during the following time(s) listed:

_____   _____

_____   _____

_____   _____

Name: _____

Child's Name: _____

Bookmarks and Incentives

Duplicate the ladybug and display one for each child. (You will need several sheets of colored dot stickers.) Let the children decorate their ladybugs with the dots, earning them for good behavior, homework completed, books read, or any other purpose for which you want to use an incentive. When a child's ladybug reaches a predetermined number of spots, offer a reward such as an extra recess or computer time.

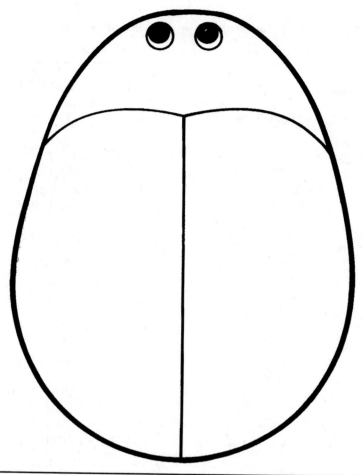

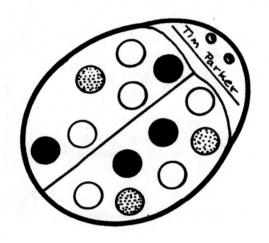

There is nothing like sharing a good book with a friend.

Get Bug-eyed and READ!

Ladybugs Up the Wall

Ladybugs have sticky pads that allow them to walk on the underside of leaves, across windows, and even up the walls! Duplicate the page as many times as you like. As a class, color and cut out the ladybugs below. Affix two-sided tape or "glue it over-and-over" stick glue to the underside of each ladybug and place them all around your classroom for fun and easy decorating.

Ladybug Calendar

Use this calendar for your lesson plans or for your children to keep a record of their independent work throughout your ladybug unit.

	Saturday					
	Friday					
	Thursday					
	Wednesday					
	Tuesday					
	Monday					
	Sunday					

Ladybug Stationery

Unit Awards

Ladybugs are
friendly,
helpful,
and good to have
around.

So are you!

To: _____

From: _____

Date: _____

Just flying by to say, "Good job!"

_____
Name

_____	_____	_____		_____
Day	**Month**	**Year**		**Teacher**

Bibliography

Anglund, Joan Walsh. *"Ladybug"* in *The Random House Book of Poetry for Children*. Random House, 1983.

Bailey, Jill. *The Life Cycle of a Ladybug*. The Bookwright Press, 1989.

Bernhard, Emery. *Ladybug*. Holiday House, 1992.

Carle, Eric. *The Grouchy Ladybug*. HarperCollins, 1977.

Cohen, Richard. *Snail Trails & Tadpole Tales: Nature Education for Young Children*. Redleaf, 1993.
Creepy Crawlies: Ladybugs, Lobsters, and Other Amazing Arthropods. Sterling Publishing Co., 1991.

Crewe, Sabrina. *The Ladybug*. Raintree, 1997.

Dorling Kindersley Staff. *Insects and Crawly Creatures*. Macmillan, 1992.

Echols, Jean. *Ladybugs*. University of California at Berkeley Press, 1993.

Fischer-Nagel, Heiderose and Andreas. *Life of the Ladybug*. Carolrhoda, 1986.

Goor, Ron and Nancy. *Insect Metamorphosis: From Egg to Adult*. Macmillan, 1990.

Halley, Lynda. *Ladybug*. Millbrook Press, 1997.

Hanks, Dr. Hugh. *The Bug Book* and *The Bug Bottle*. Workman, 1987.

Hartley, Linda. *Fly Away Ladybug*. Garrett Educational Corporation, 1996.

Hawes, Judy. *Ladybug, Ladybug, Fly Away Home*. Crowell, 1967.

Herberman, Ethan. *The City Kid's Field Guide*. Simon & Schuster, 1989.

Himmelman, John. *A Ladybug's Life*. Children's Press, 1998.

Jeunesse, Gallimard and Pascale de Bourgoing. *The Ladybug and Other Insects: A First Discovery Book*. Scholastic, 1989.

Johnson, Sylvia A. *Ladybugs*. Lerner Publications, 1983.

Lilly, Melinda. *Eye Spy a Ladybug*. Price Stern Sloan, 1997.

Lonborg, Rosemary. *Helpin' Bugs*. Little Friend Press, 1995.

Lowenberg, Heather. *Ladybug's Ball*. Random House, 1998.

McClung, Robert M. *Ladybug*. William Morrow, 1966.

McShea, Susan. *Ladybug, Ladybug*. St. Martin's Press, 1994.

Morton, Arthur. *Ladybugs, True Beetles*. Delma's Creations, 1994.

Nanao, Jun and Hidetomo Oda. *The Ladybug*. Raintree, 1986.

Oram, Hiawyn. *Creepy Crawly Song Book*. FS & G, 1993.

Podendorf, Illa. *Insects*. Childrens, 1991.

Ransford, Lynn. *Creepy Crawlies for Curious Kids*. Teacher Created Materials, 1987.

Ross, Michael. *Ladybugology*. Carolrhoda, 1997.

Royston, Angela. *Insects and Crawly Creatures*. Macmillan, 1992.

Ryder, Joanne. *First Grade Ladybugs*. Troll, 1993.

Sterling, Mary Ellen. *Thematic Unit: Creepy Crawlies*. Teacher Created Materials, 1990.

Watts, Barrie. *Ladybugs*. Franklin Watts, 1991.

Insects and Science Equipment

To order ladybird beetles and other ladybug paraphernalia for your classroom, call **Insect Lore** at 1-800-LIVE-BUG or contact them on the internet at www.insectlore.com. Only credit card orders are taken over the phone or internet. Otherwise, request a catalog. Write to the company at P.O. Box 1535, Shafter, CA 93263. Please be aware that bugs are only available at certain times of the year.

Answer Key

Page 8

1. gorilla
2. skunk
3. elephant
4. stag beetle
5. rhinoceros
6. whale
7. yellow jacket
8. sparrow
9. hyena
10. praying mantis
11. ladybug
12. lobster

Challenge: boa constrictor

Page 12

Answers will vary.

Page 17

1. sad
2. angry
3. happy
4. surprised
5. confused

Page 29

1. red and black
2. orange and yellow
3. black and gray

Page 37

Page 38

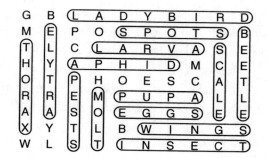

Page 40

1. $6 + 6 = 12$
2. $2 + 2 = 4$
3. $4 + 4 + 4 = 12$
4. $2 + 3 + 3 + 3 = 11$
5. $7 + 5 + 3 + 3 = 18$

Pages 41-42

The spots go in order from 7 to 17.

Page 43

The following problems add to 20 and form a path: 1 + 19; 15 + 5; 12 + 8; 3 + 17; 19 + 9 or starting with 1 + 19; 15 + 5; 20 + 0; 13 + 7; 14 + 6; 2 + 18; 4 + 16; 11 + 9.
There is slight variety to these two basic movement patterns.

Page 44

1. rhombus
2. triangle
3. oval
4. circle
5. square
6. diamond
7. rectangle
8. octagon

Page 48

1. 8	12. 4
2. 13	13. 15
3. 23	14. 8
4. 1	15. 18
5. 18	16. 18
6. 10	17. 4
7. 4	18. 2
8. 2	19. 14
9. 12	20. 23
10. 30	21. 27
11. 24	

Page 49

1. two-spotted ladybug
2. ashy gray ladybug
3. nine-spotted ladybug
4. spotless ladybug
5. convergent ladybug

Page 54

abdomen

antenna

elytra (outer wing)

eye

head

inner wing

jaw

leg

thorax (shield)